JANICE K. ROSS

Additional audio stories transcribed by Jim Nisbet

Drawings by Maddie Ross

NOT MISS WHITLAWBURN

Twinlaw

First Published in Great Britain 2021
By Twinlaw Publishing
Kirkcairn, Westruther, Gordon
Scottish Borders TD3 6NE

Additional audio stories transcribed by
Jim Nisbet
Drawings by Maddie Ross

A CIP catalogue record for this title is available from the British Library

ISBN: 978-1-9164558-1-8

www.twinlawpublishing.co.uk

REMEMBERING
DEDICATION
WHITLAWBURN
DEDICATION
REMEMBERING
WHITLAWBURN

Dedication

My dad, Rab Kielty, my hero, a legend.

In memory of dear Frank Hargrave (1962-1980) of Roslin Tower.

From *Echo* (1862)

Come to me in the silence of the night;
Come in the speaking silence of a dream;
Come with soft rounded cheeks and eyes as bright
As sunlight on a stream;
Come back in tears,
O memory, hope, love of finished years.

Christina Rossetti (1830-1894)

Front of No. 1 Aron Terrace

COMMUNITY
MEMORIES
WHITLAWBURN
STORIES
FRIENDSHIPS
FAMILIES

Introduction

In 2016, just as my first community narrative *Voices Galore* was published, I learned that 'east' Whitlawburn was to be demolished. I felt sad because I had grown up in the scheme, in fact the Kieltys were one of the first families to be rehoused from Woodlands Crescent into a 3 bedroom flat in Aron Terrace. My memories are of a vibrant new community, and I thought it would be a shame if the life stories of the first families of Whitlawburn were lost because themes of those shared experiences are culturally significant; they provide individual interpretations of how a community develops its own identity.

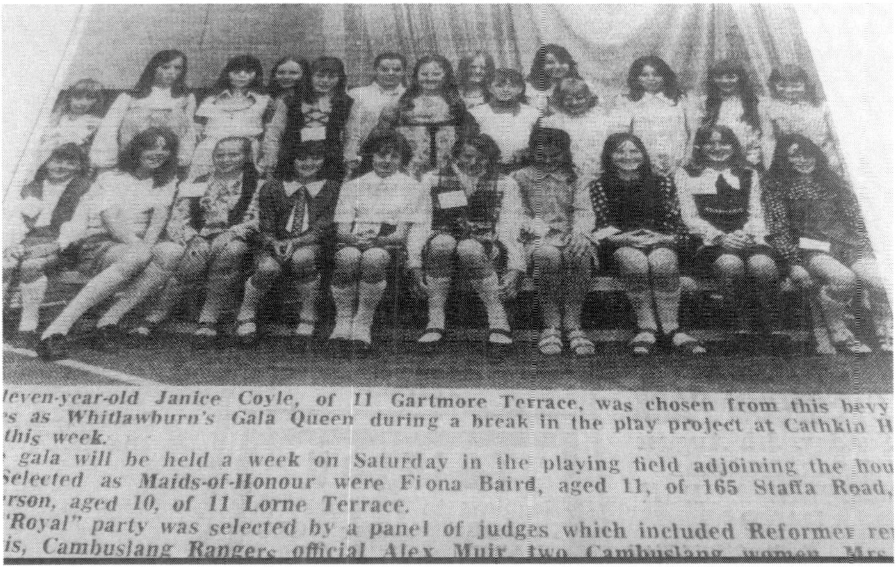
leven-year-old Janice Coyle, of 11 Gartmore Terrace, was chosen from this bevy
s as Whitlawburn's Gala Queen during a break in the play project at Cathkin H
this week.
gala will be held a week on Saturday in the playing field adjoining the hou
Selected as Maids-of-Honour were Fiona Baird, aged 11, of 165 Staffa Road,
rson, aged 10, of 11 Lorne Terrace.
'Royal" party was selected by a panel of judges which included Reformer re
is, Cambuslang Rangers official Alex Muir, two Cambuslang women, Mrs

Rutherglen Reformer coverage of the Miss Whitlawburn contest 1973.

My objective was to find members of the first families and convince them to record their memories of the scheme in the 1970s and 80s. In 2016 I contacted Paul Farrell and his team at West Whitlawburn Housing Cooperative for assistance and in a newsletter of 2017, a photograph of my mum and dad outside our old close in Aron Terrace featured alongside a short narrative describing my aims. It has taken me 5 years to get from the first recording to publication, and I am indebted to Donegal based Jim Nisbet, originally from Maxton Terrace, whose enthusiasm and transcription skills helped enormously.

From the first advert, and by word of mouth, over 20 people recorded their life story. Tales of 'doakies', newspaper and milk 'runs', of finding fun on the Asda building site, games of rounders, catching ice-cream vans, and what it was like to be in the local gang, the Maxton Bombers, feature! Some of us left and some stayed. Bridging generations, these stories are about families, neighbours, and enduring friendships.

The title refers to the local beauty contests of the 1970s, when we girls lined up in the community annexes of Cathkin High School, innocently parading ourselves in front of local dignitaries, hoping to be crowned queen of the scheme, Miss Whitlawburn! I was never picked but somewhere in the background, just audible above the hushed excited whispers, before our number was called and our fate sealed, I was singing along to the tinny sound of a feminist anthem playing on a radio.

Not Miss Whitlawburn is a community narrative. It is a 1970s West of Scotland tapestry, threaded with the stories of the first families of Whitlawburn. To those on the outside we were 'schemie' trash, living in a 'concrete jungle' but like all jungles, it was teeming with life. This book celebrates that life.

Foreword: James Kelly MSP 2007-2021

Over recent months the new housing in East Whitlawburn has begun to take shape. However, beneath these shiny new buildings there is a tale of times past, a community that came together in good times and bad, and a history that forged the lives of many people.

It is crucial that these memories are not lost and that is why we are in debt to people like Janice Ross and Jim Nisbet who have given so much time, not only to document their story, but those of so many others.

Community in those days was how people came together and the stories in these pages bring back to life how people looked out for each other. I know they will bring back treasured memories for many who were part of the East Whtilawburn area.

I grew up in Halfway and our main early experience of Whitlawburn would be our family shopping trip to the Asda. This was in the 1970s, and unlike today, Whitlawburn Asda was the only main supermarket in Cambuslang. It was a big bonus particularly for a big family like ours. There were 9 of us, my Mum and Dad, me and my 6 siblings and I used to come up with my Dad to Whitlawburn. It was quite exciting getting a big trolley and pushing it up and down the crowded aisles.

Little did I know in the 1970s that the Whitlawburn Asda would become a focal point for another poignant memory. A decade later, the 1984/5 Miners' Strike was a huge issue in Cambuslang especially with its lengthy association with coal and steel. By 1984, all the local mines had closed but there were a good number of miners still working in pits like Cardowan and Polkemmet. The Cambuslang Trades Council and the local Labour Party together collected food and money every weekend for the striking families. Often on Friday afternoons, the busiest day for the Asda, we would stand outside, and I have fond memories of joining people like Gordon Massie and Robert Ross. We received a lot of a support from Whitlawburn and other local communities.

There were several powerful voices who fought for better facilities, and one was Davie Tannahill, who had a strong commitment to the area. I recall from my involvement in local politics and community campaigns how fiercely passionate Davie was about fairness, not just for those in Whitlawburn but all communities.

People will have their own thoughts and memories. What follows is a rich collection of personal stories that tells the tale of a Cambuslang community of families, and of powerful characters who should never be forgotten.

James Kelly *MSP for Glasgow Region in the Scottish Parliament 2016 – 2021,*
MSP for Rutherglen 2007 – 2016

Contents

Plan of housing in East Whitlawburn

Contents continued

Jessie Knitting her Family together
MADDIE

Janice Ross (Kielty)

'Could the winner of this year's Miss Whitlawburn please step forward'...a sharp intake of breath... 'Janice K'. I was just lifting my foot to step forward when the name 'Coyle' was announced. My heart sank. It was not me but Janice Coyle, a worthy, gorgeous winner. I melted into the background, forever Not Miss Whitlawburn.

This is my story. I was born Janice Kielty in a tenement close in 169 Woodlands Crescent, Halfway, the third child of Jessie O'Brien and Robert Kielty. My dad was a brickie, a time served builder, a master of his craft. Mum was a housewife, a homemaker, and both built, knitted, and baked their family in 27 Aron Terrace in Whitlawburn.

Like many other first families in Whitlawburn, my parents came from the backstreets of Newton and Cambuslang. My mother's family were the O'Brien's from Colebrooke Street, later rehoused into Rosebank Drive in Halfway. My Halfway nanny, Jessie Winnie, originally came from Newarthill and had left home at the age of 14 to work as a house maid in a big house in Thortonhall, before moving to work at Cambus Court Hotel in Central Avenue where she met my pappy, who was delivering coal. Michael O'Brien was from a family of five brothers and one sister who lived in Silverbanks, but whose people had come over at the time of the Great Starvation in Ireland, they were from Dundalk.

My dad's family, the Kieltys were from Newton, and he was born in a close in Hallside village, the son of Martha Campbell and Jack Kielty. Martha, my Circuit nanny, was the youngest of fourteen children born to Mary Anne Green and Alexander 'Sanny' Campbell. She was a lovely dancer and learned Irish jigs at Jeannie Falloon's dance classes. Martha's mum, Mary Anne Green, apparently was the first female JP in Lanarkshire and a parish councillor. Over the river Calder there is a small foot bridge named in her honour, the Green Bridge. It provided an alternative safe walking path for the children from the small mining village of Caldervale (Finmeoot) so they could attend the primary schools in Newton without having to walk on the road or along the railway line. Her people, like her husband's, 'Sanny' Campbell's, were a mixture of Scottish and Irish.

Likewise, my Circuit pappy's family had, so the folklore suggests, come from County Sligo and of 11 brothers, 9 went to America, and 2 came to Scotland. Everyone I know who shares the Kielty surname is a cousin. Somewhere down the line Bernard Kielty married Helen Lochiel in Rutherglen and there began the migration of the Kieltys into Cambuslang. Both sides of the families worked at the coalfields, and later in the steelworks. My Circuit pappy Jack was born in 77 Dukes Road, where until very recently, some member of the Kielty family lived. Jack and Martha met at the dancing in Cambuslang. My mum and dad met on a Cambuslang bus run to Dunfermline, and my mum disliked my dad, she thought he was too forward, but he was a good dancer and there began the O'Brien and Kielty family, my family.

A middle child, the youngest daughter, I grew up between Karen, Anne, Robert, Eric, and Stephen. Large by today's standards, but back then it was normal, and certainly smaller than the larger families of my paternal grandmother's family. My mum likened us to members of her family so that my eldest sister, Karen was soft and doughy like my Halfway nanny, Jessie O'Brien, and my gorgeous looking elder sister, Anne, was compared favourably to her own sister Ann, an ex-beauty queen, having won the title of Miss Cambuslang. I, on the other hand was compared to my mum's brother Andy, a big bruiser, an ex-miner with a nose like a trumpet! Dad, to soften this unfavourable comparison, lovingly reminded me there were lots of lovely tall women in his family. I grew up acutely aware of my mum's embarrassment of having such a tall daughter, and as a result I always walked beside my dad.

Lots of the first families of Whitlawburn shared Scottish and Irish heritage, and many had come from the back streets of Cambuslang, so that the Bison built flats of the scheme were superior to their other homes. Cheap to build, they alleviated the council's responsibility of housing growing families. However, the downside of the flat roofed, concrete block construction materials, and asbestos lined heating systems, meant they were unsuitable. Within a short time, tenants had organised themselves into campaign groups. The Tannahills, the Lindsays, the Kieltys and others joined to improve the lot of the first families of Whitlawburn.

To those on the outside Whitlawburn was described as a concrete jungle but to those on the inside it was a new vibrant community and people respected the new houses. My first memory of the scheme was the day mum picked up the keys, and being unable to wait until the next day, she traipsed her five (my youngest brother Stevie was born in Aron Terrace) children through the Public Park when it was dark. My eldest sister Karen was pushing Eric in the pram and mum was hovering over the rest of us organising free hands with bags of stuff. At this time dad was working away on the building sites in London and had suggested to my mum not to accept a Whitlawburn house, because as a builder he knew they weren't very good, nor would they be big enough for a growing family of 8.

I was a bit scared, however mum's chatter with her friend, Mrs Paterson, made me feel safe but that turned to distress when mum started crying when she found the Western Road exit locked and chained. Our bags of stuff were weighing heavy, and Mrs Paterson told mum we could leave through the 'posh' exit at Mansfield Avenue. Trailing behind, we took care on the downward sloping path and walked underneath the dark canopy of the trees then stretched our legs up past the quarry hill where the little girl fell (now immortalised by a small monument). All too soon, we were deafened by the sounds of the rushing burn as the water cascaded, splashing over the sandstone of the small waterfall until we were across the footbridge, then finally uphill to the war monument, where we emerged unscathed from the darkness into the brightly lit avenues of the big bought houses. We passed by in hushed tones until we reached the building site of the scheme, and up into 27 Aron Terrace.

Dropping our stuff, like her little lambs we followed mum from room to room laughing as she danced with delight filling up the huge space. Newly built, the sweet welcoming smell of recently sawn wood encouraged mum as she ripped all the plastic coverings from taps and door handles. Cupboards opening and shutting, a dissonant cacophony of giddy laughter echoing as mum rejoiced at her big kitchen. That was my first night in Whitlawburn, and I don't remember how we got home but my next memory is one of carpeted cosiness, steaming apple tarts from the oven, and

Plan of a four-apartment flat in Whitlawburn, of the same style to the one Janice lived in with her parents and siblings.

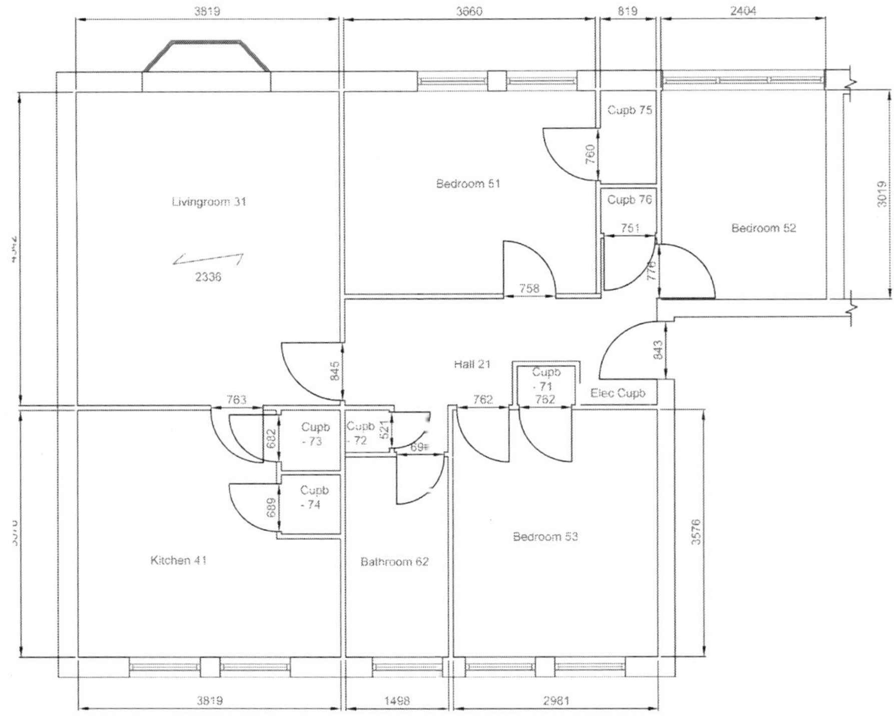

Image Courtesy of South Lanarkshire Council

"My dad was raging when he found out mum had signed up for one of the flats, it was way too small. I shared a boxroom with my youngest brother and big sister. The room was so small you couldn't fit in anything other than bunk beds and Stevie slept on a tiny camp bed. It was cramped but the huge space we had outside made up the lack inside."

watching the explosions of castles of rainbows from the *Wonderful World of Walt Disney* on our newly rented coloured telly.

Our close was lovely and clean because all the women took their turns of mopping the stairs and bleaching the chute. During the winter we pulled the front close doors shut and played on the landing for hours. Mum would give us odd squares of carpet, not a rug, only such a piece as to be of no use to anyone, and all the children jigsawed the floor coverings together and made ourselves snug. My brothers' *Action Men,* cool in their fatigues, and the suave, debonair, hollowed eyed bionic *Steve Austin* would wink to catch the attention of our pink swim-suited *Barbies* posing elegantly in their white high-heeled shoes.

Anne, my sister, made from paper towels pineapple patterned long skirts and bikini tops by tucking folds of paper around our dolls so that they could change from their swimwear into their evening dresses. We pretended to each other and to our friends that the dolls came alive and danced together but only when no one was looking, of course! My tall friend Ann, the youngest daughter of the Stewarts who lived above us, had *Mousetrap* with all the pieces, and for hours we played that along with *Kerplunk.*

Toy tills rang with the sounds of many wee shops, and fake money made us wealthy enough to choose what we wanted from coloured pictures cut from an old Kays' catalogue. Swapping scraps was my favourite and I had lots of old Mandy and Bunty annuals full of pink and blue angel sets, prettily dressed babies, wedding sets of kilted blond-haired grooms and smiling brides, and sets of untouchables whose status was marked by a clear cellophane covering to prevent sticky fingers. The words 'yes' and 'no' were scribbled on the back to indicate their exchange value. I spent hours organising my scraps in Whitlawburn. At the top of the close next to Geraldine's was a small drying room and sometimes we took our carpets there to play.

If it snowed heavily dad would get our two old metal ruddered wooden sledges from our cellar at the bottom of the close and we would gather outside the Aron Terrace pensioners' houses, then sledge down to Staffa Road. If we fell off sideways snow covered our faces making us laugh and cry at the same time. The gradient of the hill seemed steep then. Everyone joined in including mum who would leave a bit early to put tea and toast on for us coming home. Out of our wellies, cold and wet, fingers and toes stinging, we would put on our crocheted slippers. To extend the life of the

NOT MISS
WHITLAWBURN

slippers, dad had cut foot sized shapes from old linoleum and glued them on. They were warm and cosy, and our snowy fun ended with everyone watching a film, usually a western.

When the first sounds of spring arrived, we left the close and explored the space of the fields and headed for the Coosie. I think dad was instrumental in securing this as a recreational ground for the first families of Whitlawburn. Often it was used as a place to play football. A wire fence separated the Coosie from the farmer's cows in the next field. When the weather warmed, we played at tents. Made from old sheets or scabby bed spreads, of no use to anyone, we would threw them over the wire fence then stretch them out to create a triangular 'lean to' sort of shape before securing it with big stones, usually plucked loose and heaved from the side of the burn. Inside this secret world we listened to the muffled sounds of the summer, my brothers and friends playing American falls and hide and seek. Birds sang, cows lowed, and the bumbling burn flowed on by.

The tractor cut the grass, and sometimes we ran behind following its tracks. There were amazing outdoor spaces in Whitlawburn and hours were spent outdoors, refreshed by bottles of diluted orange, plain biscuits, and quartered apples and oranges. Sometimes the teenagers organised games of rounders which involved everyone in Aron Terrace. By the time it was my turn to bat my team were out, and I was a fielder. Older girls like Morag, Anne Marie, and my eldest sister Karen, were big hitters who managed magnificent runs before shouting 'stump'.

The same girls were also great at doakies. A doakie is a jump from one side of a burn to the other. A snakelike trail began just outside the Coosie and followed the downward flow of the burn before reaching the fence separating it from the cows. The jumps began with simple steps, but as the water deepened and the banks widened, they became more treacherous, until the final jump where a rope swing was needed. My sandshoes were always dripping long before the big ones swung Tarzan like, champions once again.

Midsummer was spent in preparation for the annual Miss Whitlawburn contest. To practice we held our own Miss Aron Terrace. Girls would descend to the enclosed drying area outside our close. To protect our modesty, we would place old curtains over the wooden fences, then from an assortment of old Pippa Dee dresses, Laird Porch twin sets, hats, scarves, old scuffed heeled shoes and Ann Stewart's granny's pink ballgown, we'd dress up and choose numbers. Mums were the judges, and having finished their housework, armed with their knitting, they would sit on top of cushions at the mouth of the close. Beside them were bags of needles, wool, and their patterns. As our numbers were called, we'd sashay, then clip clop from the drying green to describe our hobbies before twirling and returning to change. The anticipation of winning was intoxicating. My sister's blue velvet First Communion cape was draped over the winner's shoulder but for no more than a minute. I didn't ever win Miss Aron Terrace; I guess I was too much like my Uncle Andy.

Lazy hot days were spent playing a series of skipping ropes, elastics, balls and peever. Ropes graduated from wavy, to one and out, then bellies where the older girls jumped in fast rhythm to, 'PK chewing gum, penny a packet, First you chew it then you crack it, Then you stick it to your boyfriend's jacket, P…K…Chewing… Gum… Penny… a… packet'. At the end of each line, the final word accompanied by a quick turn of the ropes until the voices and ropes chanted and turned in very quick succession.

I wasn't any good at bellies because as I grew tall, the rope turners remained small and my head was always caught on the rope. Elastic ropes were made from elastic bands which came from the pocket of my mum's Hoover factory overall and were knotted together and joined like a rope. These then were placed around friends' ankles, knees and thighs and stretched out. The aim was to jump successfully clearing different heights, like a high jumper. With my giraffe legs I should have excelled, but I didn't.

Bouncing balls rhythmically against a wall, keeping in time to songs like, 'Oranges, oranges, four a penny; Mother's ill and she can't buy any; Father's drunk and he hasn't got a penny; oranges, oranges, four a penny' were very popular. The aim was to improve coordination by mastering a series of complicated juggling games. In Whitburn, traditional 'peever' was called 'beds' and this involved throwing an old shoe polish tin, or a stone, into a numbered square then on one foot nudging it into another square without landing it on a line between the squares. There were large slabs outside our close and it was easy to imagine them as squares to chalk in numbers. I spent hours hopping, shifting stones with my big feet.

Some weekends I would go with mum to Paddy's Market in the SaltMarket of Glasgow. My sister Anne, ever the wit, named it PM Boutique, so if mum bought her something, she would tell her friends it was 'from a little boutique in town!' Listening to the hawkers' patter was such fun. People sold anything, from odd shoes and broken LPs, it was a theatre of the streets, lanes full of culture.

'Everything for 10 pence hen, dig in, its nearly new…', its friendly atmosphere, cosy. Mum's lucky finds were pushed into green St. Michael's bags so that if we met anyone on the return journey, they would think she had been in an expensive shop. I loved Paddy's because there were lots of wee stalls to spend my pocket money on books and scraps, all for pennies. Apart from buying Eileen Ronayne's hilariously written, *Memoirs of a Tall Girl* from Scholastic book magazine in S2 English, I didn't ever buy a new book or enter a book shop until university. Proudly in my home hangs the wonderfully evocative painting *Rita's Find* by Avril Paton, and every day it reminds me of the fabulous time, space and culture that was Paddy's Market.

Some Sundays, dad, if he was flush, would take us to the Barras and we'd enjoy pink candy floss, brown paper pokes of hot sugary doughnuts and scoff like vultures while he searched an assortment of tool boxes, listening to the voices of the East End that he loved.

Sometimes mum stayed at home preparing roast dinners and knitting for her growing family. I am going to be contentious and claim that she was the best knitter in Whitlawburn. Lots of young mothers learned how to create with wool from mum's demonstrations. They learned to follow intricate baby patterns, the secrets of casting on and shaping the needles into plain and purl patterns. Mum knitted with an assortment of different sized needles using Aran, Shetland, and Mohair wool. Her family had 3 new jumpers (the boys) and 3 new cardigans (the girls) for the winter. She knitted six at a time, and although the wool was the same, different patterns reflected our age and style. One of the last cardigans she knitted for me was a pastel blue Mohair cardigan with pale brown buttons but by the time she had cast off her final stitch, the arms were too short! I had grown again! Wool wasn't cheap, and she would order a large stock from the Hosiery in Cambuslang and stretch its cost by buying it as it was needed, like 2 balls a week. Mum learned knitting at Gateside School. She was asked to bring in wool to learn to knit socks. She felt ashamed she had no new wool and had to unravel her brother's old discoloured jumper. She was no good at knitting socks but developed great skills to keep her children cosy and warm. As I write, she is still busy counting her stitches.

In all the years I lived in Aron Terrace she organised the same weekly meals: Sunday was roast silverside; Monday, leftovers; Tuesday, mince and potatoes; Wednesday, homemade vegetable soup and sweet rice pudding; Thursday, stew; Friday, lemon sole bought from the fish van which sat across from the Asda entrance in the carpark of Benmore Tower. One day when I was off school I went with her to buy fish and said ' yuck fish again', and received a real telling off from the fishman who asked me if I knew how much it cost to buy 8 slices of the best fish! My beetroot face meant I never disparaged again. When Asda opened in 1975 my mum was delighted because it saved her having to go to Cambuslang for her messages.

Before Asda opened, a mobile grocer came on a Wednesday afternoon. 'The wee mobile', sold groceries around Whitlawburn. He drove around the terraces and sat at the back of the closes while all the women and children queued waiting to be served. On a Friday a white Askit van came selling similar produce, in addition to lovely fresh cream cakes. Occasionally after school, if mum wasn't feeling good, I would be sent over to the Cathkin bypass to cash mum's Family Allowance in the post office then buy potatoes, milk, and bread from the Co-op. And always a wee treat for going!

Most Saturdays, my sisters and I would be organised and sent to Cambuslang to purchase the weekly groceries from Curley's which sat in the middle of the Main Street. I think it is where Kolor King is now. A long list which included slabs of butter, cut wired cheese, mum's favourite Ayrshire bacon, an assortment of tins and cream and plain biscuits, eggs, and tomatoes. Heaving string bags, we entered the butchers for silverside, square sausage, stewing steak, and potato scones then went next door to the green grocers for apples and oranges in brown paper pokes, and potatoes wrapped in newspaper. The highlight was choosing the weekly comics from RS McColl's - Bunty for Karen, Jinty for Anne, and Mandy for me, Roy of the Rovers, Beano and Dandy for my brothers and as my sisters grew older the Jackie, Blue Jeans and Mates were chosen. We would wait for the 21 bus outside Shafer's, and dream of the latest boutique fashions.

Asda killed off the bustling shops on Cambuslang's Main Street, however, it provided easier and cheaper access of much needed resources for the growing first families of Whitlawburn. And, it became our playground. We watched its construction, and for the free juice and biscuits we attended its opening night. A year later Mum won a competition for Camay soap, and the reigning Miss Scotland, the gorgeous Carol Grant, came to our house in Aron Terrace to deliver the 20-bar box prize. We were all thrilled and remained loyal customers to Asda.

By the time I went to live in Whitlawburn I was 7 years old, so St. Cadoc's was my first school, and St Anthony's my second. It was a bit of a trek to get to school from Aron Terrace because I had to walk the length of the scheme, through 3 new underpasses before emerging at Springhall. Then it was across a busy road, past the shops and Cathkin Library before a quick run along Lochaber Drive. It took half an hour most days. Sometimes if dad was 'snowed off' he would run us in his old grey van which had a starting handle. At 5 minutes to 9, he was still turning the handle and pulling chokes, and we'd get behind to push it up onto Morven Road, chugging it to life. We were then all in the back, giggling, knowing he would never let us down. We always picked up friends and neighbours, dad's motto was 'there was always room for one or two more'! Most days the long journey was filled with skelping ropes off the pavement, bools rattling in my brothers' pockets, and the happy companionship of family and friends. Long cold winters were days of icy slides and snowball fights; summers of newly lawned grass and buzzing bumble bees escaping from our clover filled jars.

Inside, school was a cheerful process of learning, and I loved the miracle of new sounds and words. I could easily express myself and glowed when asked to read aloud in class. In a big family, small steps are often forgotten, so I loved my classroom achievements. Words constructed new worlds, and I still rejoice in their power to do so. However, I stumbled over the ordered rules of writing stories, even with the help of Fuzzy Felts. Eventually I caught up, but I still find it much more difficult to write words than to read them. But in the safe cosy world of St. Anthony's and Trinity, making mistakes was fine, practice always made perfect.

Apart from the world of words, I loved the magic of fine tracing paper, and what you could learn from copying other's work. I won a prize in an art competition by tracing a canoodling couple from the front cover of one of mum's Mills and Boon books. My entry followed an elaborate process: I traced the outline then carefully turned it over, placed it on top of a blank sheet of sugar paper then gently scribbled the indented pencil marks to recreate the image. Once coloured in with a few broken crayons, I drew in a new background with a bright yellow moon then handed it into my teacher who sent it off. A few months later, to 27 Aron Terrace a huge brown tube was delivered with my name on it, and its arrival caused quite a stir because no one knew I had even entered an artistic competition. Its guts soon spilled out onto the kitchen table, I had won a prize of a personally signed print of a real artist's painting and a letter of commendation wishing me luck with my future artistic endeavours! My sister Anne, after hearing about how I had prepared my entry, noted that they probably only received a few entries! But it was what school gave me, a window, to glimpse different identities from those of Whitlawburn.

When I was 10 in Miss Butler's class, brimming with confidence after receiving praise from her friend for my reading, a deeply blushing little robin redbreast, I was asked to accompany Miss Butler on her journey home and carry her big brown leather bag. Aglow, I chirped all through the underpasses, feeling so special until the junction of Langlea Road directed us into different worlds. The memory makes me smile because I realise it wasn't about me, it was just that she was terrified of being attacked, and having her bag stolen! I find it strange when I hear of people expressing how frightened they were walking to and from school, I never ever felt scared. I loved school, and Margaret Kyle was the best primary teacher ever, and I am so glad I was able to thank her for the wonderful contribution she made to my life.

In my final year at St. Anthony's, for the first time I stayed away from home and spent 3 weeks at St. Columba's residential school. Set in the rolling Border hills of Newton St. Boswells, this old seminary introduced me to the beauty of the environment. In a world antithetical to Whitlawburn, its space assaulted my senses, so full was it of flora and fauna in its natural habitat. After long meanders by the River Tweed I slept soundly. Two special activities took place: one was being shown into Sir Walter Scott's house in Abbotsford, and the second was learning to swim at Galashiels. It was great fun. The school is now a business centre and the current janitor is the son of the 1970's housekeeper, and he remembers the bus loads of 'schemie' kids coming to stay. I know this because a few years ago, on my way to play at Kelso Folk Club, I arranged a visit and he shared his life story while showing me around. Afterwards he opened the old chapel and I played a few tunes while listening to the ghosts of my childhood.

I hated leaving the cosy warmth of St. Anthony's to attend Trinity High School. Its large size and huge pupil numbers made for an unpleasant transition, as did the change in route. As there were no specially timed buses for pupils from Whitlawburn, the good half hour's walk from Aron Terrace meant that if it was raining my learning process often began in soggy tights and sodden shoes. In my final, very rebellious year, I wore trousers underneath my skirt and was sent home by Mr. Quigley, the headteacher. But I had great teachers at Trinity, and those who stand out were my English teachers Christine MacPhail and John Wilson (forever A Man For All Seasons); my

Chemistry teachers Andy Bancewicz and Frank Daly; Des McGuire of the Drama department and the wonderfully eccentric but hugely talented music teacher, Jack Hendry. Their influence was always positive and friendly.

When I look back, I was lucky to be young at a time when there was real positive investment in the infrastructures of communities, and during the summer holidays, we had a Playscheme to attend. Set up by community stalwarts like the Tannahills, and other members of the Whitlawburn Tenants' Association, we were given the run of the new community school, Cathkin High. One of the newest, and by far, best comprehensive schools built in Scotland, it catered for community needs and included a swimming pool, 3 gym halls, a games hall and athletics track. It was a wonderful space, and every day we could, we attended, and tried new games and learned to trampoline. Funded by council and charity grants and run by a series of volunteers from the scheme, it was one of the success stories of Whitlawburn because it was a space of constructive learning. Community minded people like Betty Lindsay, Nessie Tannahill and Molly Keery, everyday gave up their time to make sure its community participant model provided much needed inspiration to the scheme children. Arts and Crafts were my favourite and I lost count of the number of misshapen, grey glazed ashtrays mum was gifted. It was a great environment to grow up in and it provided a structure to the long summer holidays. It cost pennies, included great bus runs, and I, and my siblings, greatly benefited from it. Other publicly funded activities included Morven Road's summer entertainment of Punch and Judy. Old-fashioned seaside entertainment right on our doorsteps. On the grass verges we laughed at the old patriarchal interaction then marvelled at the magician. Street theatre always brought a feeling of happiness.

Sometimes the ragman would come to the scheme. His voice and discordant van horn immediately sent everyone scampering into their homes to search for old clothes, all for a balloon on a stick! There was something magical about the Ragman because money was never exchanged. It was the only van where that happened. In the evenings the catchy jingles of the resident ice-cream vans Pelino and De Marco cheered up many evenings as we queued for cones, wafers, single and double nougats, MB bars, Spangles, Marathons, Salt and Shake crisps, Space Invaders, Pink Panther pink chocolate bars, Toffos, sweet tatties and lucky bags.

There was a mobile fish and chip van and I worked on that with my friends Emma and Peter. I helped chip the potatoes on a machine in Emma's kitchen in Mount Vernon, then put them into a big black bucket. Peter organised the fish then we headed to Whitlawburn. Once the van stopped in the car park of each terrace, our tasks were clear - Peter battered the fish, Emma deep fried the chips and I organised the salt, vinegar, sauces, and paper. For a time, the van was popular. Dad came out one evening thinking he might run it, but he realised it was difficult to keep the frying oil warm while driving around. After we gave up the run, Whitlawburn got its own permanent mobile chippie which sat across from the Bel-Air.

At the car park of Cathkin High School, the shows came. Every year they brought an exotic flash of colour, smells, and sounds. Candy, floss and apples, sugary dummies on coloured ribbons, doughnuts and mouth-watering hot dogs were scoffed. A small amusement arcade, a clever thief of many saved pennies, promised great prizes that were never won. There weren't many rides but the high-flying Chair-o-planes and the Speedway brought gorgeous excitement and short-lived fearful thrills. Looking through time, as if it was yesterday, a brief glimpse shows me the bravado of teenagers pushing each other up the steps of the Speedway and onto the soft velvet seats of the motorbikes. Marc Bolan sang how it was to boogie on a Saturday night as the lights flashed and the boards pounded faster and faster. One night a dare didn't go so well. Paddy Coyle, big brother of Janice of Miss Whitlawburn fame, decided as the Chair-o-planes swung faster and higher into the fading sun, to remove his safety chain. As he waved below to everyone, he fell to the ground. Forever remembered as Icarus of Whitlawburn, a man of great showmanship.

I was always involved in performing shows for my family and friends. I wanted to be a great actress and tread the boards. I attended the junior school at the then Royal Scottish Academy of Music and Drama. I would come home from school, have dinner, change, then run to the Cathkin bypass to catch the bus. I adored all the classes. For 2 years this was my routine until I moved to Glasgow Arts Centre in Washington Street where there was a more working class feel to the drama. I acted in a play called *Sweetie Pie* alongside Blythe Duff and Justin Currie from Del Amitri, but the highlight of my acting career came about when I was cast as the Wicked Witch of the West for Trinity High's production of *The Wizard of Oz*.

What I won't ever forget about the academy, was the wonderful sound of orchestral instruments tuning up, and my huge desire to learn music. The only instrument we had in our home was a comb and paper. Until a strange coincidence took place.

It involved the Saturday morning jumble sales which the Tenants' Association held outside at Morven Road, just before Maxton Terrace. I, along with others would go round the scheme, up and down the towers, collecting jumble. At this time my sister Anne had started judo, and among the jumble she found a judo suit. She donated 20 pence and was so delighted. Fast forward a few weeks, and already growing bored with the pushes and falls, my sister spotted, while watching Noel Edmonds' *Multi Coloured Swap Shop,* someone in Sheffield who was wishing to swap a Spanish guitar for a judo suit. The judo suit was packed up and sent on, and for the first time ever, the Kieltys had a musical instrument! Like the judo, my sister quickly tired of it, but I persisted. From Cathkin Library I repeatedly borrowed *Play Guitar Today* and learned the basic chord formations to sing along to Bob Dylan's *Blowin' in the Wind* and *The Sloop John B*. I think I drove everyone mad!

Although I love making music, and still play guitar and fiddle, I am not very good. But like everything, learning is a lifetime's journey. Recently during the first 'lockdown', I saved both a cello and piano from the Cambuslang dump. I am now learning to play them too. It is how I spend my time. Strangely, once the piano moved into my home, I found out that mum can play piano by ear. Having no instruments in Whitlawburn, she didn't ever get a chance to develop her skills.

My friends in Whitlawburn were Lydia 'Teapot', Evelyn, Shirley, and Marie. Lydia, Evelyn, Shirley, and I were friends from primary and we would swap scraps and play dolls. Lydia 'Teapot' lived in the next close in Aron Terrace, her big sister had been a former Miss Whitlawburn. We had lots of fun swimming at the Dolan Baths in East Kilbride, and attending Girl Guides every Friday night in Springhall, laughing, and giggling in our black hats and blue uniform. I used to go on day trips with Evelyn's family when her father was home from the oil industry, where we would spend a day camping. I took my own breakfast, sneaked out the fridge, of one bacon rasher, a tattie scone, an egg, and a square sausage which Evelyn's mum later cooked outside their tent.

We had some fun times before they moved to the Wimpey estate across the road from the scheme. Shirley came from Cathkin, and sometimes we would play at her house instead of the scheme. She was friends with Steven and Sandy, and I remember we all went to the cinema to see

The Spy Who Loved Me. I accompanied Shirley's family to Butlins in Minehead and we were best friends for a few years. We puffed our first cigarette when I was 13 and became work colleagues at the Savoy bingo when we were 14. My friend Marie lived in the towers, we met at secondary and shared some of the same classes. During the summers of the early years at Trinity, we would save our bus fares, walk home through Cambus ang Public Park, sooking blocks of cola flavoured ice, which were Kwenchy Cups from a freezer, and laugh at all the teachers. I stayed overnight with Marie on quite a few occasions listening to Rod Stewart until all hours. Our mothers had grown up in the back streets of Cambuslang and we always, even to this day, trust each other. We went to Hampden to wave tartan scarves at Ally MacLeod and the Scottish team, our heroes, as they flew off to Argentina to bring home the World Cup!

Like Ally's heroes a lot of the Whitlawburn boys wanted to be famous footballers. My brothers were part of the dream, they were bound for glory. We all believed talent could propel any ordinary boy into superstar status. Robert and Eric played for Cathkin United before joining East Kilbride teams. As they grew, they both played at junior level and once played against each other in a local derby of Cambuslang Rangers against Rutherglen Glencairn. This may have been the year when Eric was awarded 'Player of the Year' for Rutherglen Glencairn. Jock Barkey who managed Cathkin United was their hero and his passion for the sport encouraged all the young boys to play their hearts out on the field.

Dad became a real live hero and saved a man's life. Mr Stewart, from the flat above, chapped my dad's door and told him one of the pensioner houses was on fire. Fitter and faster, he ran downstairs, out the close, and like superman kicked the back gate and door open. Covering his mouth with his jumper, he lifted the unconscious man over his shoulder and brought him to safety. The national press noted his heroism, but they referred to dad as 'Bob', and we all laughed because no one ever called my dad 'Bob'. Dad always played down his superpower heroics, claiming anyone would have done the same thing.

I used to babysit for a lot of Whitlawburn families, and I met my first boyfriend when Shirley and I were sitting outside Evelyn's close at Gartmore Terrace. This was next to my Auntie Elizabeth's where I was due to babysit my niece Jennifer. My auntie was always so vibrant, and kind. She was knitting me a long brown wool jumper which I was really looking forward to. A daughter of Mrs

Paterson, who had accompanied my mum on our very first visit to Whitlawburn, she had been married to my dad's brother John. One summer evening just before my babysitting duties started, Shirley, Evelyn and I were spotted by 3 lads cycling their way round the scheme. They looked so cool, pedalling their racers with no hands. That was the day Frank and his friends came into my life. After giggling goodbye, we ran upstairs to my aunt's and from her top flat window we could see the boys waving at us from Frank's 6th floor bedroom window in Roslin Tower. In the months that followed, the sweet thrilling magic of first love filled my every waking moment. Until tragically, on our way home from a friend's home in Halfway, the motorbike we were riding, crashed, instantly killing Frank. Physical breaks heal but the consequences of a head trauma remain. In the aftermath, I failed all my school exams, and spent the next few years self-destructing.

I left school just as the Thatcher years were beginning to bite, and the young people of Whitlawburn felt the impact of the loss of employment opportunities in the Hoover, Redpath and Clydebridge works. Giros became a way of life for many young people.

At this time, I left Whitlawburn for pastures new. Within three years I was back living in the homeless flat in Morven Road, with a baby daughter. With family support I found a job, was

Janice aged 15

Janice and her dad.

Janice and her mum.

Janice and her mum and dad.

Janice, her brother Robert, sister Anne and Geraldine McGaulley at the Coosie

rehoused into a large 4 apartment house in Cathkin, and then enrolled as a mature student at Glasgow University.

Growing up in Whitlawburn shaped my life. In 2016 when I found out my old home was about to be bulldozed, I felt sad. Sad because there was no record of the vibrancy of the first families of Whitlawburn, no mention of those who shaped the identity of a community that everyone was proud of. Ordinary people sharing their life stories in their own voices is a rich cultural tapestry. An oral history sewn together by the threads of an insider's unique experience and perspective. I have loved recording and listening to all the stories.

In the early days of Whitlawburn, the newly formed Tenants' Association organised a befriending group where young people were encouraged to visit pensioners. I was a befriender, and it was my responsibility to visit and chat to Mrs Holt and mum's older, retired work colleague, Chrissie, two doors down. I loved their stories. It is a huge shame their voices and experiences are gone forever and that's why it is important to record life stories of ordinary people. I was fortunate I was allowed back into our old flat before the bulldozers flattened it, to record mum's story. To be the first and last person across the threshold was very poignant indeed.

Opening the door of 27 Aron Terrace was stepping into a deep tunnel of time. Mum's voice transported us. And there we were, laughing loudly as dad folded old newspapers into pirate hats, and mum knitted her family together. A first family, of the community of Whitlawburn, so full of the promises of tomorrow.

Adam Donaldson at the door to his Aron Terrace flat.

Adam Donaldson

I lived in No. 11 Aron Terrace with my mum and sisters, Morag and Jean.

My great-grandfather was a mining engineer who moved from Bo'ness to Halfway. At the turn of the last century both places were full of pits. My grandfather was also a mining engineer and he started a fishmonger business for his wife to run which did pretty well. My uncle Davie continued to run it up until the 70s. He had two shops and a fish van that travelled around Cambuslang, Cathkin, Springhall and Whitlawburn. My father had a sweetie and comic shop in Halfway which was a child's dream. My mother had no connection to the locality, having been brought up in the Gorbals and Pollok area.

When my parents married they first lived in the pre-fabs at the bottom of Mill Road, Halfway (where the Scottish Specials are now) before moving to a two-bedroom house in Springhall.

My mum was quite thrilled to get a house in Whitlawburn. Although our house in Springhall was only about ten years old, Whitlawburn was brand new and a step up because of the extra bedroom. However, the small bedroom set above the close entrance was always freezing as the hot air heating system never seemed to reach the far end of the house. There was also a funny aroma around the house, like a new car smell, that lasted for ages.

The cellars at the bottom of the close were disgusting. There was a "midge room" where large items of rubbish such as boxes and furniture, that couldn't fit in the waste disposal chute, were stored pending collection by the dustbin lorry. I can't count the number of times this room was set on fire. Afterwards, my mum and other neighbours had to join forces with cloths and mops to clean the smoke damaged walls of the close.

There was also communal consensus that everyone took their turn cleaning the stairs on a rota basis. A card with all the house numbers was put through your letterbox on a certain day. This system went back to the days of the tenements – a simple way of reminding you that it was time to do your bit.

Whitlawburn was right on the edge of the city – the last stop saloon before East Kilbride. After Whitlawburn it was just fields in the 1970s.

Neighbours in our close included the Simpsons, us and directly above were Chic and Danny Doherty. There were also the Reids and the Wallaces. During the 1970s the Orange Walk started in Morven Road, apparently because the father of the Wallaces was high up in the organisation. I'll never forget being woken up on Saturday mornings with the bandsmen tuning up outside our close.

In the first close in Aron Terrace was George Russell and his twin brothers, Joe and Gary, who were a year older than myself. Their father worked with my mum in the Hoover factory which employed half of Cambuslang, manufacturing washing machines, irons and vacuum cleaners. The Russells had a caravan in Anstruther as did my dad, so it was the same friends I played with on holiday as I did at home when the Hoover closed down for the Glasgow Fair fortnight.

I also hung about with James and Charles McAuley from the next close, the Kielty brothers Robert, Stephen and Eric, and Michael Mullin from Morven Road. I was also pals with Garth Westland who had been brought up in America – he was probably the most exotic thing we had been exposed to at that time. We'd regularly jump on the No. 21 bus to Rutherglen where we joined the Cubs and, later on, the Scouts which I attended for many enjoyable years.

We all played in the field in front of Aron Terrace, a great place where your parents couldn't see you. I remember trying to fly my kite here and running backwards into the goalposts, splitting my head open! Someone once dumped a dozen or so 50-gallon oil drums and we had a wonderful time playing with them, building forts and playing doakies. On one occasion, there was a gala day held in this field with stalls and games – a summer fete sort of thing.

There was a play area out our back between Aron Terrace and Maxton Terrace, but we never really bothered with it. It was just a concrete slab square with big lumps of metal in the middle - one was a climbing frame shaped like a rocket and another resembled a set of goalposts. Outside the front was another square with two big rocks. Typical 1970's council – gave you some concrete and stones to play with! I think there were more than a few injuries caused by those play parks.

The shows used to come during the summer in the 70s. That was a big thing, even though there were only four or five rides and a few stalls – imagine, a funfair coming to Whitlawburn!

I went to school at Loch Primary in Springhall. That was quite a hike from Aron Terrace. It was about a mile and I hated that walk in the mornings.

If you wanted to save yourself the walk, there was a wee coach that picked up pupils at Morven Road and elsewhere in Whitlawburn and dropped them off at the Loch and Saint Anthony's schools. It cost 2p for the trip. I don't think there was anything official about it, just a guy with a coach looking to make a few bob.

Adam Donaldson at 15

I later attended Cathkin High which was built around the same time as the scheme. It was basically a big concrete lump but was well-equipped with gyms, a swimming pool and a large library. I've always enjoyed reading, so I spent a lot of time there. The school doubled as a community centre for the locality and had a theatre with lots of shows. A dental practice also operated within its walls, although it always seemed to be a different dentist. It was only in later years I discovered this was a training ground for budding dentists who had recently qualified to gain experience of mouthly matters.

However, my clearest memories of Whitlawburn are of open spaces, the burn, the tree swing, playing soldiers up at Johnny's Woods – great places to be adventurous and throw yourself about as young boys full of energy do. I still remember being bawled at by my mum: "Have you been down the burn again," and bringing out the nit comb from the kitchen drawer!

Alex McLaren

Alex Mclaren

I was born in the pre-fabs in Halfway. My family then flitted to Cathkin when I was four. We moved to Whitlawburn in 1973 during my last year at primary school. I can't recollect the month, but it was around the time the young boy from East Kilbride was murdered in the underpass connecting Whitlawburn and Cathkin. I had to walk from our new house in Lorne Terrace to Cathkin Primary and I remember the underpass being closed.

Lorne Terrace and Staffa Road were the last houses to be built in the scheme. We lived in No. 21. When we first moved in, we had fitted carpets and felt dead posh. In Cathkin it was just lino on the floor. I slept in the "cupboard room" which was two above the close entrance and was always freezing as it was also below the drying room on the top floor which was just concrete. The blow air central heating system rarely reached the end bedroom.

I remember looking forward to the primary school trip. My dad and uncle had arrived back from Anstruther with a load of mussels which were cooked in a pan with vinegar. During the night I took no' well but knew if I was heard going to the toilet to be sick my mother wouldn't let me go on the trip, so I was sick out my bedroom window instead. Returning from the school day out, my mother asked: "Were you sick last night?" "How did you know?" I replied sheepishly. "Take a look outside," she said. On the front wall of the building was a bright, pebble-dashed stain running directly below my bedroom window. Caught!

After Cathkin Primary, I headed to Cathkin High School. It was a good school and had only opened a few years before I went. My sister Kay went there too. I was in Telford House. The other houses were Kelvin, Livingstone, Stevenson, Napier and MacIntosh.

I grew up with a lot of good people who lived around Lorne Terrace and Staffa Road. In the first close, as you came from Rona Terrace into Lorne, were Steven, David and George Lloyd and the Scotts, Graham and Elspeth. In the second close were William and Sylvia Copeland and Lee and Linda Brough. Next, in the third were the Grants, Allison, Arthur and John and the Bullochs, Jane, Jamie and Margaret. We lived in the fourth close along with Drew Hamill and his sister Morag. In the fifth close were the Pattersons, Fay, John, Linda and Denise with the Clarkes, Ann, Mary, Margaret and David. In the last close were Jacqueline, Lorraine and John Shearer. In the first close of the two-blocks in Staffa Road were Ailsa and Morag Farmer. In the second were the Smiths, Michael, James and AnnMarie. Others in Staffa were the Jones, Danny, Chic and Liz; the Irvines, John, Ann and Myra; Donna and Pauline Toner; the Wards, Gerry, Mick and Libby; Harry, Joe (Boney) and Lisa Hughes and in the last close Fiona, Heather and Allister Baird.

Me, the Bullochs and the Grants all used to hang about the monkey puzzle or play doakies and one-man hunt at the burn. We'd sometimes dam it up and we flooded the new houses a few times! No one ever got hurt. The only incident was on the swing when someone cut through the rope. [Think this may have been Edward McGaulley from Aron Terrace who broke his leg, circa 1973. JN]

The burn ran all the way through Whitlawburn from the Coosie in front of Aron Terrace and Staffa Road to Lorne Terrace, where it disappeared into a tunnel running parallel with Western Road, then under Greenlees Road and into Cambuslang Public Park. We would walk through the tunnel into the park. Arthur Grant was the tallest and had a pair of waders. At the deep bits he used to give us all a "cokey."

I remember the Playscheme during the summer holidays and trips on the grey bus – the 'windae-licker' bus – to places like Glasgow Zoo. Molly Keery [Rona Terrace] and Betty Lindsay [Maxton Terrace] ran it. Betty did a power of good for the community. Mrs Brownlee [Morven Road] used to help now and again.

We were all part of a big community. There were Gala Queens and football competitions in the park. We'd sometimes camp out there and get up early and steal the milk from people's doorsteps for devilment. We had dens in the cellars and collected ginger bottles to trade at the ice-cream vans that toured the scheme, such as De Marco and Pelino. There was also the visit of the shows now and again where you could try your luck at winning a goldfish at various stalls or looking cool by jumping off and on the Speedway. One incident springs to mind was when Paddy Coyle flew off the Chair-o-planes and narrowly missed a truck.

My father worked in the steelworks and still resides in Whitlawburn in the pensioner houses. My mother worked in the Bel-Air for many years. She served the pub-grub in the function lounge upstairs. It was nicknamed the "Stab Inn" because every other weekend someone got done in!

There were a few gang fights, mainly between the Whitlawburn Skull and the Fleeto from Halfway. One night we were fighting down at Lorne Terrace, chasing the Fleeto along the grass back in the direction of the park. The 'polis' came and we ran towards the underpass at Western Road. They drove right to the side of the tunnel and we ran to the back close, but it was locked. They caught two or three of us and put us in the back of the van, drove us through the Public Park and dropped us off at the swing park at Halfway and told us to walk home. That was our punishment!

I got married in 1987 and moved across the road to Holmshill, so I was still in the vicinity. I've seen a lot of changes, especially after they knocked down the Circuit and moved all the "dafties" here – this just brought Whitlawburn down. It's quite sad that [part of] Whitlawburn has been demolished. If it had been built right in the first place they wouldn't have needed to pull it down. It was substandard and the flats were full of dampness. It's not just seeing the concrete going, it's your childhood memories. It's sad to think of all the people that have passed away like Jimmy Coyle, Gary Lindsay, Mick Gourlay and Morag and Ailsa Farmer

I'm now back in Halfway. It's not that far from Whitlawburn, but it's a whole world away from where I grew up.

Alison Gilmour

Alison Gilmour

I moved to Morven Road when I was about 11 years old, just before I went to Cathkin High School.

We lived in Tobermory Road in Cathkin until I was two and before that in the pre-fabs in Cambuslang when I was a baby. My mum (Nancy) and dad (Harry) were from Silverbanks and Westburn – Cambuslang born and bred.

Whitlawburn had been up for a few years before we moved. I remember all those new houses being built and my mum saying at the time we needed to put in for one.

Me and my brother, Scott, were growing up a bit and we needed separate rooms, so we were really chuffed when my mum told us the family were moving to a four-apartment in Whitlawburn.

There were a lot of nice memories of growing up there.

I used to go about with Karen Kielty. I remember us being out one night with two local boys from Aron Terrace and winching in the bottom of a close. My dad was very strict, and I had to be in at nine o'clock on the dot or he would be shouting from the window which was a big embarrassment for me. However, the lad I was with had deliberately put his watch back half an hour, playing for extra time. Meanwhile my dad was wandering all over the scheme looking for me! It was all different then, but what my dad said went.

I used to babysit for John and Eileen Docherty [Maxton Terrace]. They had two boys, Kenneth and Stuart. It's what you did then, and I enjoyed it. I never took money, but they used to buy me things.

I had a paper round which was passed on by my brother. I didn't want to do it as I thought it was a boy's job and I got slagged at school because I was a girl. But my dad said: "Look, you get a fiver a week and it's all yours to do with what you like." I thought of all the things I could buy – I really loved my clothes – so I said I'd do it, but I refused point blank to take the big paper bag with "EVENING TIMES" splattered all over the side. So, my dad got me a message bag instead and I carried that around. Wee Willie Allison (wee Five O'clock) who lived up the next close used to help my brother and he knew the run and list of customers. He came out with me until I settled into the routine, but I hated it. Still, at least I got to know Whitlawburn. My mum had a Goldbergs' account. That's where I got most of my clothes when I was young. You paid it every month or quarter or, if you wanted a big item, on the budget account.

I was also friendly with Ann and Esther Stewart in Aron Terrace; whose mum had a catalogue and I used to get wee things like perfume which I could pay up with my paper money.

When I moved away from Whitlawburn, I felt unsettled, but when I moved back there was a sense of home. I was in Clifton Terrace and then bought my brother's house in Cathkin. After we sold up, I was in Lorne Terrace, then Albany Terrace and finally in the new houses in the fields where the Coosie once was.

Things have changed so much – different buildings, different atmosphere, though I think if anything happened people would still pull together.

I don't think I'd like to stay anywhere else – I'm quite happy here in Whitlawburn.

Barbara and Esther Stewart

We lived in no. 29 Aron Terrace and had moved from my granny's in Kings Crescent, the Circuit. When I first moved to Whitlawburn it took a wee while to settle in but eventually I got to love Whitlawburn as did my mum and dad.

My dad liked looking out at the view across the green fields to Kirkhill golf course and beyond to the Cathkin Braes, but eventually that all went as more houses were built in the fields and down along the burn towards Staffa Road.

My granny took no' well and came to live with us until she died. She was my mum's mother and was a Stevenson from Newton. I think her mother came from the north as my granny could speak a few words of Gaelic. It was a bit crowded in the house and I had to sleep on the couch, but as a family we were all very close.

There weren't many amenities in Whitlawburn. We used to play tig or on the swing across the burn and tennis out the front. I remember my granny used to have a big pink ballroom dress which we wore when holding Miss Aron Terrace beauty contests in the drying area. There were no DVDs, nor Nintendo but we were all happy.

Everyone was so nice to each other, and we had great neighbours and great times as kids. Some of those who lived in our close were Peter Simpson, Geraldine and Alice McGaulley, Betty and Dennis Henderson and the Kieltys. We all got along. We would sit out the front at night for a chinwag and sometimes Peter Simpson brought his guitar and we'd have a wee singsong. I think most people in our close were Cambuslang people and that helped to cement a sense of camaraderie and build a community spirit. That seems to have all gone now.

When I left school, I worked in Asda in Whitlawburn for about a year. Before Asda opened everybody did their shopping in Cambuslang. You'd get a bus to Cambuslang's main street and then a taxi home with your messages.

My mum's favourite shop was Mackays where we would get all our school clothes. Other shops were Shaffars, Curleys, Stepek, the Co-op and Hasties. Then there was the Salvage Store which used to sell broken caramel wafers and digestive biscuits and various damaged stock which smelled of smoke. The shop was fire-damaged and black inside, but it didn't stop us from going in. My dad wouldn't go near the place. I remember buying a tin of bashed paint from the Salvage Store and gave it to my dad. He asked: "Did you get that from the Salvage Store?" "Naw," I replied. "I dropped in on the way home." "I'm not painting my house with that!" my dad roared.

While in Asda I'd put my name down for a job in the Hoover factory in Cambuslang. I worked there for 7-8 years and it was heavy going but the money was good. My dad, mum, Uncle Alex and cousin Nelson all worked here. There were two factories – one was for manufacturing washing machines and the second factory produced carpet hoovers and irons. (Barbara was also employed, soldering wires for washing machines, but took redundancy in 1981. She had bad asthma and the dust was affecting her health.)

That's the way it was. You left school and there was almost full employment and you could pick where you wanted to go. But all the industry has gone, and Cambuslang became a sort of a ghost town when Hoover closed down.

Both of us later moved to Clifton Terrace across from Cathkin High School. (Esther moved to Shawlands after her daughter was married.)

A lot of Glasgow's overspill moved in when Whitlawburn was brought under control of the city. I saw the old Whitlawburn disappearing. I remember one time being scared of going to the shop because of eejits hanging about outside, drinking, shouting and swearing. It was never like that when we were young and to say you were scared in a place where you were brought up is a big change.

I don't miss Whitlawburn, but I do miss the old Whitlawburn.

Betty Baker

We moved to Whitlawburn to Morven Road in 1983 with my husband and son and daughter, then aged 9 and 3. There was not much for the kids to do, we had helped with the youth club in Cathkin so we asked if we could access the small hall used by the pensioners on Morven Road. They were not happy but eventually they agreed to share. I went to the cash and carry to buy some tuck with my own money.

We put up posters on the hall and shops advertising the club to be open on a Thursday night. We charged 50p at the door and played music. There was a pool table and a tuck shop. That was the start of the club, then we started having a Friday night disco and that went down really well. When I think back to the memory of us walking with our television and video down Morven Road on a Saturday morning so the mums could leave their kids to go to Asda to shop.

We had fancy dress nights and with the money we raised we took the children on day trips to the seaside. There were a few of us involved in this, Davy, Marian, Bob, Joe and his wife. We had some great fun times and it gave the children a place to go.

MAXTON BOMBERS
(JNR BRIGADE)
RIP
Johnny's Woods

Derek Watt

I moved to Whitlawburn with my mother and brother David in 1972. I was about two years old. We lived in No. 4 Maxton Terrace at the corner of Morven Road, which seemed to be the main place where everyone met.

It was a great place to grow up. I made friends quickly: Shug McGuinness and his wee cousins, Brian and James McGuinness, Robert Galloway and the Drummonds from the towers. I still see some of them to this day.

One pal was Willie "Five O'Clock" Allison from Morven Road. His dad and mum managed the Bel-Air, the local pub. Back in the early 70s, the pubs shut in the afternoon until early evening, and it was the only time they could get home to make his dinner. Every day without fail, his mother would shout out the top flat window: "Willie, it's five o'clock – dinner time," and unfortunately for him the name stuck!

I'll always remember the people, the faces and all the dogs in our close. Betty and George Lindsay lived next door with their four sons, Geordie, Jim, Jock and Gary. Other neighbours were the Hetheringtons, Kevin Scott, Doris Baker and Mrs Liddell who lived up the top. The dogs were Shep, Judy, Patch and my dog King.

My mum was always sitting out the front with her friends – it was a good community. My mum came from Colebrooke Street in Cambuslang, and she told me the reason why people were so close was because they mostly came from the backstreets of Cambuslang. When these houses were demolished many moved to the new builds in the scheme. My uncles, John and Hughie Evans also stayed in Whitlawburn.

The Maxton Bombers were a group of older youths from around Maxton Terrace and Morven Road. They weren't really a gang; it was more camaraderie - just a bunch of friends who gave themselves a name. Think they must have been into the Bay City Rollers at the time, as I recall them wearing tartan on their clothes. We younger boys were the junior bombers or the Wee Bombers! There were never any mass brawls or anything like that, but you knew if you were in trouble there was a close circle of friends around you.

We moved from Maxton Terrace to Aron Terrace in the 80s, but as mum got older and the stairs in the close became steeper, the council offered us more suitable accommodation in Eastfield where I presently live.

I attended St Anthony's Primary School in Springhall. It was quite a walk to St Anthony's, but you never walked alone, always with friends. It was quite intimidating going through the tunnel between Springhall and Whitlawburn when you were young especially with graffiti proclaiming: "The polis work has been in vain – the Skull Boot Boys have struck again!" The Skull was the local gang and was an amalgamation of the Cathkin, Springhall and Whitlawburn teams. That's why school friends could come and go between each other's schemes without much fear.

Religion was never something that I remember being spoken about when I was growing up in Whitlawburn. Obviously Celtic and Rangers were spoken about and I had friends that went to Loch Primary. I knew my friends who went to Loch followed Rangers but was never aware of why, it was accepted as it was, and it didn't have any effect on my childhood. I think I became aware of it when I started secondary but after school it was left there. The Orange marches would sometimes start and finish in Whitlawburn but there was never any trouble or fuss.

Once, while walking home from school, I found a fiver. My mum took me down to Asda and bought me a big bar of chocolate. I remember the day Asda opened. It was all brand new and we got cakes and orange juice. My mum went to the cigarette kiosk and there was a photographer standing there who took my photo. I'll never forget the blinding flash.

The new store saved all the women from having to go to Cambuslang and having to catch the number 21 or 72 bus back up the road. Before that my mum used to take me to Safeway in Burnside for her shopping. Asda was a godsend. For us boys it was a wee money-making enterprise. We used to ask shoppers: "Can I take your trolley back? Can I take your trolley back?" Most of them would say: "Aye," and give you a wee bit of silver.

Growing up in Whitlawburn there weren't many amenities. We would go to the Playscheme in Cathkin High School during the summer holidays to use the gym, swimming pool and do Arts and Crafts. Sometimes we'd go on bus runs to Saltcoats or Burntisland and it all cost buttons. If the Playscheme wasn't on, we'd go up the Coosie (the cow fields) and play football. But the sport of kings was "kerby" where we spent hours throwing a ball across a road.

I remember Brian McGuinness and myself made a golf course right round the scheme. It was 18 holes and started and finished in Morven Road. Basically, we just entertained ourselves.

We'd also spend the day playing on the big rope swing or doing doakies all along the burn from Staffa Road up to the dual carriageway to East Kilbride. Across the other side of Western Road was Johnny's Woods where we would make dens. I had a cat that died when I was about five or six years old. Some of the Maxton Bombers held a funeral procession and buried it up in the woods.

I really enjoyed going walks to Dechmont Castle. Back then it was all fields; now it's all houses. On one occasion the cows escaped down Morven Road and one even made its way to Asda. Sometimes we'd cut across the fields to Kirkhill Golf Course to collect ginger bottles to trade at the ice-cream vans that toured the scheme. They were Pelino, Gogi and De Marco, who used to give us "brokies" – the broken wafers and sweets.

One hot summer, Mr Kielty from Aron Terrace built a swimming pool out of four large planks and heavy-duty plastic stuck together and filled by a hose. It was unbelievable. Weans appeared from everywhere to put their toe in it and even the adults came just to have a look at it.

The shows would often make an appearance in Whitlawburn. This was a small fairground with stalls, dodgems, the Speedway and the Waltzers where everyone would hang about. I remember one night when Paddy Coyle fell off the Chair-o-planes The shows were situated opposite Bute Tower in the car park next to the Bel-Air but ended soon after they built houses there.

Another pastime was a trip to the towers. You could slide open the lift doors with a piece of metal and stop the lift, then climb on the roof for a ride. There was an extension at the rear of the lift, used for transporting coffins, and you could stand on that and rock the lifts - scary stuff.

My favourite stunt was climbing from the verandas into the bedrooms on the towers. First time I did it was in my pal Jim Patterson's flat on the 11th floor. We were playing cards one night and I was winning hands down, so they locked me in the bedroom. Looking out the window I thought I could reach the veranda, so I opened the window, grabbed on to the veranda, swung out and climbed over. When I chapped the living room window, they all started screaming. I got no credit for it or any round of applause, just a mouthful of obscenities and abuse. Crazy the things you did when you were young!

A young Derek Watt with Santa

When it got dark we would play football wherever we could. Underneath every terrace block were garages, gable ends and on wooden boards in huge letters "NO BALL GAMES" signs. There was a good-sized bit of green behind where I lived in Maxton Terrace and it had a pole with "NO BALL GAMES" but we would use it for a goalpost because no one would complain about us playing football there. Once when it was too wet to play on grass we had a kick around in the communal drying green and I jumped over a shopping trolley but being so tall I hit a washing line with my neck and fell back with a thud. Got more of a fright than anything else but learned a lesson that time.

Whitlawburn has been a place that was always being built on as far back as I can remember. It seemed that when the scheme, the flats and towers were completed, new Barrett houses were built across the burn from Staffa Road. Then we got the Asda store across the road from the Bel-Air. Then the Salvason estate was built on the other side of Western Road. Then the flats got a makeover and slanted roofing added. Then the towers got cladding. Then the last bit of green space (our football field and Coosie) got a new estate built on it. Then, when there was nowhere left to build, they pulled our half down ready to start again. Whitlawburn may have changed its look many times but my happy memories remain unchanged.

Back when CB radios were popular Whitlawburn was known as "The Concrete Jungle" and it was obvious why.

Eric Kielty *Janice's younger brother*

I was born in Halfway but moved to Whitlawburn when I was a tot. I lived in Aron Terrace from 1971 to 1985. These were fine times, and I had a great upbringing and grounding in life.

There was a brilliant community spirit in Whitlawburn.

I remember neighbours sitting conversing at the close steps during summer, jam pieces being hurled out of windows for you and your pals, my dad building a makeshift swimming pool out on the front green, the big swing over the burn where someone was always guaranteed to get a sore one, and heading over to Gilbertfield Castle or up to the reservoir at the Cathkin Braes to hunt for birds' eggs.

One recollection firmly ingrained in my mind is hearing our window creaking open followed by a piercing whistle and the call: "Right, it's 9 o'clock!" This was my dad's signal for my brothers and sisters to stop whatever we were doing and come in. We'd all troop up the stairs moaning: "Why are we always first, eh? Why is everyone allowed to stay out and play?" Then it was plates stacked high with toast and cups of tea before bed. My mum must have used about four loaves a day feeding us kids. Even to this day when someone whistles on their dog in a park my head turns round ready to head up the close!

Yet, another thing that triggers my memory of Whitlawburn is the smell of freshly cut grass and tractors mowing the huge green space out front, while we ran behind trying to catch bumblebees in newly washed jam jars filled with clover plants.

I had loads of pals. My first friend was Michael Devlin. We started school together at St Anthony's. Others were Harry Wallace, wee Joe Spiers in Maxton Terrace behind us, the Gormans, the McCabes and James McGuinness, all out playing team-handed.

One favourite adventure was heading to "the golfy" at Kirkhill to pinch golf balls. We'd hide under the fence and grab any balls that didn't land on the green, gather up a heap over a few weeks then sell them back at the clubhouse car park.

One year there was a Pro-Am tournament at Kirkhill where golfing legend Lee Trevino was one of the celebrities. Some of us local boys went up to caddy hoping to make a few bob and I got picked by Frank McGarvey who played for Celtic. At the first hole he took a sixteen, the worst score ever in the Kirkhill course's history. After the round he called me over and said: "Here's a pound wee man. Wait there and I'll bung you a few more," before disappearing into the clubhouse. He never came back. All my mates were getting tenners and I got bumped by Frank McGarvey! Years later I met him at a golf outing in Shotts and jokingly pulled him up about it. He was courteous enough to apologise and bought me a pint.

My dad and Peter Kerr started one of the scheme's first football teams – Whitlawburn Thistle. I remember scoring my first ever goal in the Coosie. I must've been 100 yards offside but the referee awarded it. We were getting tanked about 20-0 at the time by a team from East Kilbride and he must've felt sorry for us. I was also sent off for the first time at a game in the Coosie for uttering a few profanities while colourfully questioning a poor decision by the official. This was a bit of a "riddy" as my mum and dad were watching from the sidelines.

Whitlawburn Thistle was mainly all local lads. I also played for Cathkin United, who had the pick of the players from Cathkin, Springhall, Whitlawburn and Fernhill. Jock Barkey ran it – a phenomenal member of the community but known to tell the odd white lie. Once he tapped into our dreams by spinning a story that he'd arranged for us to play a few games in Germany. He'd chartered our own private plane with Cathkin United in big letters on the side and Franz Beckenbauer, the Bayern Munich captain, would meet us at the airport. "Gerd Muller wanted to be there too but he couldn't make it," he would add. "Brilliant Jock! When are we going?" we'd all exclaim. "Just keep paying your 50p every week…"

The first medal I ever got was with Cathkin United. I don't think we won anything as we were pretty crap. Jock probably bought it just to make the team feel good about ourselves. There was also a popular Friday night disco in Cathkin High School to raise money for the club.

Cathkin High was a thriving centre after school hours with classes and sports. There was even a dental surgery which I used to attend. During school summer holidays there was a Playscheme run mainly by local volunteers such a Betty Lindsay and Molly Keery. We enjoyed trips to Loch Lomond and sails on the *Maid of the Loch*, all for 25p with a packed lunch thrown in – what a bargain!

I remember Asda opening its doors in 1976 and helping my mother up to Aron Terrace with about a dozen bags of shopping. It was amazing to see this large superstore in the middle of the scheme. Asda employed a lot of Whitlawburn women and a lot of local money was ploughed back into the shop. The downside was that the previously thriving Main Street in Cambuslang took a bit of a hit and many long established shops died.

When I was about 8 years old I got caught shop-lifting in Asda. The target was a huge, hexagon-shaped box near the tills, full to the brim with Mars Bars. My pal Harry had a pair of blue and yellow wellies into which he'd tuck his jogging trousers, then stuff about twenty Mars Bars down the front. Standing at the entrance waiting for him to emerge I asked for one to which he retorted: "Go and steal yer own!" However, I'd always the fear that my dad would leather me if I got caught.

For weeks I looked on while my mates pilfered to their hearts content and stuffed their bellies with sweeties. Eventually the temptation was too much to bear. So I tucked my trousers into my socks and started shoving chocolate down my trousers and walked out. What a buzz that was. But Mars Bars weren't my favourite – I was a Fruit Pastille kind of a guy, so I turned my attention to them, and I became more and more adventurous. Whenever I was on the way home from school I'd pop into Asda and buy something, but always make a beeline for the Fruit Pastilles.

Unfortunately, our crime spree came to an end when one of us got caught by the store detectives, we were all hauled into the office, the police arrived on the scene, our mothers were called down and *The Great Mars Bars and Fruit Pastille HEIST* was all but over.

Whitlawburn was a brilliant community and I'm still in touch with pals I ran about with back in the day, but it's sad to think that old community spirit is gone. Though one thing I'll never miss is my dad's whistle at 9 o'clock!

Under construction in Whitlawburn

Morven Road flats.

George Lindsay

My mum, dad and brothers Jock, Jim, Gary and I moved to Whitlawburn from Cathkin about 1970. We lived in the first close in Maxton Terrace, and it was a good close with great neighbours like the Watts and the Hetheringtons.

Cathkin High School had just opened to serve the new scheme and surrounding locality, it was a huge community school. Starting there was a great adventure and a chance to expand your boundary and meet new friends from different places. I went about with John and William Holmes from Westburn, Derek Muir from Halfway and Alex Hutton from Springhall. It meant I could travel to these areas and no one would bother me as I had friends there.

There were gangs, and local rivalries sometimes spilled over into fights in school. Cathkin, Springhall and Whitlawburn were all under the Skull; Halfway had the Fleet, and there was the Fernhill team, but if you weren't a troublemaker or a fighter it was usually safe to go to other schemes. We just minded our own business and mucked around, so me and my friends were okay and safe enough.

When I was about 13 or 14 years old, I had a milk run along with Bill Scott and Jim Allan. We covered most of Whitlawburn. It was tiring at times, having to rise at 5am before going to school and was hard graft carrying crates of milk up the high flats and up the stairs of closes. But it was good money and you had your tips on top, as well as a few extra customers. We'd constantly be nicking bottles from each other's runs to meet the demand for our skins on the side!

I'd always money in my pocket and it saved my mother having to fork out for my clothes and the likes. On pay day the three of us would head to the Station Café in Cambuslang for milkshakes, then it was into the town or Woolworth's on Cambuslang's Main Street to splash the cash on whatever was in fashion. It could be flared trousers or records that we had heard on *Top of the Pops* that week. I was big into Slade, Sweet and Black Sabbath in the early 70s. Once we were in a record shop and I asked for Slade's recent Christmas hit. The shop assistant informed me he'd only one copy left to which big Bill Scott barged in front and said: "I'll have it!" So, we headed up to his house in Arkle Terrace to listen to it. However, halfway through the record was scratched and kept repeating "Merry Xmas, Xmas, Xmas, Xmas…" served Bill right!

Mostly we kids were out in the fresh air, playing football from midday to midnight on the square above the garages under the glow of the floodlights from the high flats. Sometimes we camped out over in the park or spent evenings playing in Johnny's Woods. One favourite pastime was to sit behind the wall at Asda with a fishing rod. Attached to the hook was an old wallet or purse which was placed on the path leading from the store. A customer would emerge, trolley piled high with messages and notice the bait. Thinking it was their lucky day, they would abandon the trolley to bend down and pick up the purse which was suddenly hooked away. Then in total disbelief they'd look up, just in time to see their weekly shopping hurtling down the slope to the car park.

My mum, Betty, and father, George were very community orientated. My dad worked in Clydebridge steelworks and mum had a job as a dinner lady. This had its perks. Betty would often come home with trays of chocolate and caramel cake and jugs of custard. Sometimes it seemed as if half the scheme were getting fed from our kitchen. She knew a lot of friends were struggling, so an extra meal now and again for their kids, and a few pence for the ice-cream van, helped, even if it was in a small way.

Being a new scheme, there were few facilities with nothing much to do and as Jock, Jim, Gary and I all had different friends our flat was an open house every single day. My mum I suppose thought she had better do something or her living room was going to be overrun. So, along with Davie Tannahill and others such as local councillor Bunty Gunn, she helped create many changes, basically to keep the mob out of her house!

Gala Days were organised, and an annual five-a-side tournament took place at the Coosie, where all the streets and towers entered at least one football team. The winning side was presented with a cup and medals by the Gala Queen, Miss Whitlawburn. Maxton Terrace won it every year and with players like Derek and Willie Stibbs, Jim and Jack McGuiness, Jim Nisbet, David

Hetherington, David Watt and the other Lindsay's in the street, John and David, we had no shortage of talent.

During the summer school holidays my mum realised there was nothing for the kids to do, so she managed to get a Playscheme on the go. At one time it was in the special needs centre in Langlea Road.

Everything cost a penny – your orange juice, your chews and even trips away for the day to exotic locations like Coatbridge for an Its A Knockout contest. However, the older ones amongst us liked a wee fight now and again with the locals, so sometimes we'd have to get a police escort out of a place. I can still picture Betty, who was the height of nothing, trying to get between these big guys and shove them back on the bus!

Then there was the time the bus, we must have been down Ayrshire, stopped next to a field full of tattie-pickers. Seeing that we were on a grey, special needs bus, they started pulling faces, shouting insults and making abusive gestures at us. We managed to get the doors open, burst out of the bus and ran into the fields after the tattie-pickers, who fled for their lives! I don't think they'd ever make that mistake again or shout at kids with special needs. The day usually ended with everyone heading back to our house, where my mum would get the chip pan on and feed the multitude as usual.

All in all, Whitlawburn was a friendly place and my mum was a real community champion. She cared about the people and place she lived in and her spirit probably rubbed off on me in my work as a professional carer. These were the good old days when much good was done in the scheme on a voluntarily basis, everyone pulled together and gave their time freely. It's a shame so much has changed.

At its peak in 1974 Hoover employed 5600 people before the final production line employees ceased work on Friday, July 22, 2005, as the line moved to China. The closure brought an end to the 49 years association with Cambuslang. Many Whitlawburn residents worked in the factory either full-time or part-time.

Geraldine McGaulley

My mum, my two brothers, Edward and Jamie, and I moved into number 31 Aron Terrace around 1971. I was about ten years of age.

I still live in Whitlawburn in Bute Tower and work as a coordinator in Whitlawburn Resource Centre on the Recycling Project. My brother Jamie stays in Arran Tower and my daughter lives nearby in Belmont Road.

My mum was originally from Colebrooke Street, Cambuslang and my dad came from Blantyre. They settled in Hallside until my dad passed away, then we moved to a one-bedroom tenement in Halfway, situated where the Sun Inn car park is now.

It was hard going for mum to bring us up. She worked in the canteen in the Hoover plant, in Camp Coffee, as a quality controller in Long John distillery and in schools. Her last job was in Hastie's factory in Cambuslang. Mum didn't have a lot, but she always made sure we went on holiday every year, even if it was only a caravan in Lower Largo, Fife.

Our house in Aron Terrace was on the top floor. This offered fantastic views of Greenlees Farm, Kirkhill Golf Course and the Cathkin Braes. It was lovely, especially if the fields were white with snow at Christmas time.

Across the landing were Liz and Paddy Hamilton and downstairs were the Stewart family and Linda and Peter Simpson. Mrs Stewart would often send me to Asda with a big shopping list and on my return, I'd get 50p, a fair amount of money at that time. On the second floor were the Kieltys and Betty and Dennis Henderson. I used to babysit for Betty and Dennis, so she could pop off to the bingo and Dennis to his darts and dominos. That was another wee earner. Garth Westland with his mum and grandpa stayed on the ground floor and next door were Hazel and Billy Cochrane with their two boys.

Whitlawburn was good then. I was friendly with Anne and Karen Kielty, Charlotte Coyle and Anne Marie McAuley who both stayed in the adjacent closes. Anne Marie McAuley's dad drove the Jacobs' biscuit lorry. I loved visiting her house as there were always loads of chocolate biscuits.

As pals, we all seemed to just stick around Aron Terrace. There was a sense of freedom with the fields in front that other streets never enjoyed. At our back sat Maxton Terrace. The only view the residents there had was of us in Aron Terrace.

We made our own entertainment. Now it's all computers and mobile phones. On the square, we played rounders, kick the can and "shops" using dock leaves for money. We'd build tents in the drying green and dress up and have Miss Aron Terrace contests. There wasn't a swing park in Whitlawburn back then. Someone made a makeshift swing from a tree over the burn near Staffa Road. It was some height and I never dared to go on it. My brother Edward broke his arm when the rope snapped.

Summers were summers then. We'd fill old washing liquid bottles with water and skoosh each other. Anne Marie McAuley, who was a few years older than me, would walk us all for miles over the Cathkin Braes to the reservoir. I remember getting chased home by a bull a few times! Sometimes we would go to the swimming baths in East Kilbride, spend our bus fare and walk back.

On other occasions a bunch of us would go plundering. We'd head down to Westcoats where the large sandstone villas were, sneak into the gardens and steal apples from the trees. Often, we'd chap the doors and ask, but there was no excitement in that. I remember getting hunted and jumped over a wall only to land in a bed of jaggy nettles. On one occasion I ate so many apples I was as sick as a pig and threw up in Charlotte Coyle's bath!

Another highlight during summer was the arrival of the carnival in the car park next to Cathkin High School. It was filled with caravans and lorries, stalls, waltzers, dive-bombers and dodgems. Anne Maire McAuley's shoe came flying off when she was on the Chair-o-planes and landed in the candyfloss stall! That was hilarious.

At Halloween a gang of us would tour the towers. I'd dress up as Mrs Mop so that my mum would give me a fag as part of the costume. I'd just started smoking then, so afterwards I'd tell her the cigarette got broke or wet, but I'd always smoke it.

Nowadays everyone wants to know where their kids are, but back then in Whitlawburn we didn't have a care in the world!

Geraldine McGaulley with Jessie and Rob Kielty

Jessie and Rob Kielty, Janice's mum and dad, outside their old close.

Jessie Kielty

If I remember rightly, we moved into Aron Terrace in September 1971.

We were living in a flat in Woodlands Crescent, Halfway when I accepted the offer. My husband was working away at the time – I didn't even ask him. I thought: "Well, this is best for us."

I had to organise moving our belongings before we moved in and many nights were spent travelling through the Cambuslang Public Park late at night.

Our son, Eric, was only 9 months old and Mrs Patterson, our neighbour in Woodlands, would babysit. So, we used to fill his pram high with stuff and hurl it through the park. It was an experience if nothing else.

I was always away ahead of myself. By the time it came to flit, everything was hung up in the cupboards and we only had the furniture to deal with.

I was friendly with the sister of John McArdle who worked for a milk company. He let us use his milk float to shift our furniture. It was cheaper than hiring a van, and you were lucky to have enough furniture to fill a van anyway.

That was the start of our life in Whitlawburn.

After leaving the flat in Woodlands it was brilliant. All we had there were two white sinks and a ring and a boiler. Now we had cupboards like we never had before, and we didn't need to buy any wardrobes for the bedrooms. Nowadays with all the technology you wouldn't give it a second thought, but back then it was fabulous.

My husband didn't want to take a house in Whitlawburn, but afterwards he loved it, as did the kids with all the fields in front of us, not like now. We had a freedom that we didn't have in Woodlands. It was a safe environment and we could see the kids at the burn or out the back, playing

Not Miss Whitlawburn

Hearing that some of the houses in Whitlawburn were due for demolition, stopped Jessie and Rab Kielty's daughter, Janice, in her tracks.

She is writing a book of memoirs titled Not Miss Whitlawburn© about her life growing up in Aron Terrace. The Kielty family, (Karen, Anne, Janice, Robert, Eric and Stephen) moved into Aron Terrace in 1971 when Whitlawburn was just being built and have many happy memories living there.

It is those memories which prompted the idea of creating a Whitlawburn Cultural Heritage Project. Janice is looking for anyone who is interested in sharing their stories, memories and photographs.

The overall aim would be to create an art exhibition celebrating the happy times of the play schemes, bus trips, local beauty contests and the endless games of 'doakies' played on the burn.

This project is open to anyone who lived in Whitlawburn and all ideas and suggestions are welcome. The first meeting will be Monday, August 28th at 12 noon in the café at Whitlawburn Resource Centre. If you can't make it and want to contribute please leave contact details with Geraldine at Whitlawburn Resource Centre and she will pass them on to Janice. (i)

Jessie and Rab Kielty outside the close in Aron Terrace where they lived.

How Not Miss Whitlawburn began

tennis. My husband fought to get a football pitch in one of the fields and even built a temporary swimming pool one summer. Children came from everywhere to dip their feet in it! They were good days.

Most of my new neighbours were Cambuslang families, though we didn't know many of them beforehand. There was Betty and Dennis next door; up above were Mr and Mrs Stewart and their daughters Ann, Barbara and Esther; across the landing from them lived Peter and Linda Simpson and on the top floor were Liz and Paddy Burke, and Alice McGaulley and her children Eddie, Geraldine and James. Alice had been brought up in Colebrooke Street, the same as me before moving to Halfway.

Below, on the ground floor, were older residents, Mr and Mrs Campbell, and Mr and Mrs Garth, who came from Farme Cross. Mr Garth's wife went through the mill health wise, so whenever she was in hospital, I'd invite him up for Sunday dinner.

I'd always a certain affinity with the older ones – I always learned something from them, and I loved going on the pensioners' days out to places such as Peebles and Berwick. I was also involved in the Tenants' Association with Davie Tannahill, Mrs Whiteford and Betty Lindsay, amongst others.

Our kids loved Whitlawburn. Our girls would dress up with their pals and hold Miss Aron Terrace contests in the drying green, while our boys were involved with football teams such as Cathkin United and clubs in East Kilbride.

The Kielty family at Whitlawburn.

50 years on, Jessie's
still knitting...

During the school holidays, there was the Playgroup Scheme funded by Strathclyde Regional Council to bring activities into Whitlawburn for the kids.

When the Asda opened in the mid-70s, it raised the quality of life in Whitlawburn. It was a godsend. Not everyone had cars then and we no longer had to stand and wait for buses to go to Cambuslang for our shopping. I remember winning the Camay Soap competition and glamour girl Carol Grant, who was Miss Scotland 1976, came to our house. It was a big thing in the scheme –people were easily entertained then!

On summer evenings, we'd sit outside at the close and Peter Simpson would bring down his guitar. We had some great laughs and there was never any carry on. All our neighbours got on fine. I'd spend many a day sitting at the close steps, busy with my knitting and talking to neighbours – I couldn't do without my knitting and would take it everywhere on day trips, trains and buses.

When I was brought up in Cambuslang this was the done thing. Mothers sat out the front and children played round about. They all looked out for each other's kids.

I worked on the twilight shift (6pm – 10pm) in the Hoover factory in Cambuslang and this suited women with young families who couldn't work during the day. It's not like that today where mothers work full-time. People have massive mortgages to pay and seem only interested in their own lives and don't mix as they used to. It's a crying shame, because it makes life an awful lot easier.

It felt quite sad to leave Whitlawburn. We were there for 13 years, but it's all part of life's journey. I always wanted my own back and front door with a garden to hang out my washing. In Whitlawburn we had communal drying greens. Having a big family, I had to ask neighbours if I could use their poles. That was life in Whitlawburn. So, it was great to look out my window and see my washing blowing in the wind in my own garden.

I loved my time in Whitlawburn, but I'm not sad to see it being bulldozed. They're renewing the place – you've got to look forward all the time.

Jim Hannaway and Janice.

Jim Hannaway

I only lived in Whitlawburn for under a year. I was 6 years old when we moved from 'the Halfway' up to Whitlawburn. When my mother told me, we were moving to a new house it sounded like she said 'Whitleyburn'.

Mum told me we were moving to Bute Tower into a high flat. I was so excited at the thought of living hundreds of feet above the ground.

We all went up in a taxi, which was very rare, to meet Mr Forsyth who was the caretaker at Bute Tower. It was the first tower completed in 'Whitleyburn'. He lived in No. 1. We were to be shown around another flat and he got the keys for No. 3. I was a bit disappointed that our flat was going to be on the first floor.

It was a great move for me, and almost 50 years later I can still recall many days in 'Whitleyburn'. It had a lasting effect on me.

For me, at 6 years old, it was a space age experience. 1971 had just arrived and we were moving into a home of the future. The heating was all electric, everything was brand new, two good-sized rooms, a brand-new kitchen and a living room with a veranda. Even then I wondered at our good luck, just a pity we couldn't see too far from the veranda though!

I learned to ride my bike in the car park of Bute Tower. It was a Saturday; my uncle was there because he and my dad would have been going over to the Cathkin for a pint. My dad got me to sit on the bike, balanced me, gave me a great big push and then let me go. The tarmac carpark was new and very smooth, and I kept my balance and there and then I was riding without stabilisers. I remember my dad smiling and me proud of what I had just done. What a feeling!

At that time the second tower, Arran, was also being let but the others were not complete or opened yet. I had a friend on the eighth floor in Bute Tower and another friend on the second floor of Arran Tower. We used to meet on the walkway outside the flats. We climbed the walls, walked along them and dreeped off the high bits. A lot of times we cycled up the walkway to Ailsa Tower. This was the top of the hill and we would challenge each other to race down to Bute Tower again and repeat until we had enough.

The tenement flats, the low risers were still in the ground, unbuilt, when I moved in. They started to take shape while I was there, and I loved the adventure of having a major building project right on my doorstep. There was so much to do and explore and very little stopping us from wandering around the developing structure of the new flats which were starting to take shape.

'Whitleyburn' was the definitive boys adventure playground for me. The site office was roughly where Asda later stood, where shops are now, and was accessible to us after 4 or 5pm. My friends and I would wander in and marvel at 'workie' tools, and all the gear lying around and try on the hardhats which were way too big. I mind my dad warning me not to lift anything out of there and made me take back a screwdriver I acquired!

Sometimes we got into trouble. One time, three of us, all six years old and street wise, were in the ground level of the Clifton Terrace flats. All around us was just concrete walls and open

The Asda store (and their trolleys) which so many remember as making a difference to their lives.

stairways about one storey high at the time. Our mission, as ever, was all about finding things to climb, jump over and dreep down from.

We found a small, square, water-filled "pit" in the ground level. It was about 6 feet by 6 feet and roughly 15 inches deep. So, we placed a plank of wood across it. I made the first attempt to walk from one side of the plank to the other. It was obvious, to anyone but us, that the plank would snap when I was halfway across. It did crack and I dropped a little at first, then it snapped, and I dropped into the pit. Splashing into the water I thought "I'm ok I have welly boots on" but the wellies were maybe only 12 to 14 inches high. The water being deeper poured in over the top of them. I landed on my left foot, wobbled and can still see the water lapping over the top of my boot. It filled rapidly as I lost my balance and placed the right foot into the pit to save me from toppling over completely. It too filled up with water. I waded to the edge and climbed out. Sat on the ground and poured the water from each welly back into the pit.

The long woolly socks I was wearing were soaked through. I remember being worried as my mother always took a dim view of my adventures. I was always coming home caked in mud and one time even lost a shoe in "quicksand" left by the workies. It slipped off as I pulled my foot out of the mud hole. They were "school shoes" too, just a day old and I never got that shoe back. This would be the last straw and I was terrified. I tried to dry out but had to go home as it was getting dark and I headed up the stair.

We didn't lock our doors during the day then and I opened the door fearing a slap from my mother. I was met by my dad and he asked me what had happened. I told him the story expecting mum to appear and give me "what for" for "being stupid" and getting soaked. But it was Saturday and she had gone to her waitressing job at the County Inn. My dad told me to take the socks off and go and get ready for bed. No fuss, no shouting. I had got away with it. I am sure we even watched a war film that night. A joint pleasure my dad and I shared.

At the end of the day this was nothing in the grand scale of life, just another kid's 'Whitleyburn' adventure but to me it remains special. I had been outside for hours with friends, exploring this amazing playground and had also learned about checking the strength of wooden planks before trusting them with your weight. We were just a few kids, barely started in life but with a barrowload of shared outdoor experiences. A wet ending was nothing and avoiding the retribution from my mother only made it better!

I moved away from 'Whitleyburn' around November 1971 back to the Halfway to a house near my gran and grandad. Later, I got to play in 'Whitleyburn' many times with my cousin who lived in the flats in Maxton Terrace. Happy days spent there too, and I remember that it never seemed to rain in 'Whitleyburn'!

Jim Moore

One of my earliest childhood memories of Whitlawburn was flitting from our old home in Benmore Tower to Lorne Terrace. I was only a couple of years old, but I can still picture my dad and his mate wheeling our belongings through the streets of Whitlawburn courtesy of a few borrowed Asda trolleys.

My family resided in Lorne Terrace from 1987 until 2001 when we moved to Springhall. However, I felt there wasn't the same sense of community that existed in Whitlawburn.

We stayed in a close with decent neighbours. There was a nice garden at the front and everyone was house proud, each neighbour taking turns to sweep and wash the close and cellars. I can still picture my mum busy on the stairs with her mop and old-fashioned metal pail.

During the summer the women would sit out at the front with their wee haufs. In fact, that was the first time ever I tasted alcohol when I mistakenly picked up a glass of whisky thinking it was Irn Bru!

This side of Whitlawburn was great fun. Later, those days all but vanished as new tenants moved in and old neighbours moved out. The junkie replaced the woman who looked after the close and the garden. A good neighbour makes things a lot easier, but when you have horrible ones it makes life so much stressful.

My first few years at school I attended Whitlawburn Annex and had a load of pals. Then, we went to Loch Primary. I always remember a sort of schism between us Whitlawburn ones and the Springhall pupils when we first arrived. It was the same when we progressed to Cathkin High School. There was a wee Whitlawburn cabal, but that disappeared when new friendships were formed. Still, you knew your Whitlawburn associates would watch your back, even though you might be knocking lumps out of each other at times.

Cathkin High was easy enough to get to, but Loch Primary was a fair mile-and-a-half from the far end of the scheme. Schoolmates all walked together and we didn't think anything of the distance. Now I work as a teacher and I see pupils being dropped off at school when they only live a few blocks away.

There was a tremendous sense of space in Whitlawburn. You were never stuck in the house. We'd always find ways to amuse ourselves. Pals would walk all the way to East Kilbride swimming baths or ride our bikes all the way to the Hoover factory where there was a bike dirt track. Sometimes we'd travel up to the Cathkin Braes. There was a whole lot of freedom.

Kids nowadays are glued to screens and that takes a toll on their mental health. They have few outlets to let off steam or any face-to-face interaction. Back then, even if friends were away on holiday or grounded, there was always somebody to hang about with.

One pal had a pool table which had no legs, so once again Asda's trolleys were utilised as a base and set up in the middle of the swing park. Sometimes a dozen or so of us would pitch a tent on the grass between Lorne Terrace and Staffa Road and camp out overnight. Then we'd rise early to go and steal the milk from the doorsteps. Once we got a tray of doughnuts at the back of Quicksave. That was a real good score.

Often I would spend all day doing doakies or playing football with the squad. Many places didn't have doakies and even some of the patter is different, they don't know what a "doakie" is. We were lucky having the burn flow past Lorne Terrace and an ideal place to play doakies. One doakie involved jumping about 15 feet over the burn from a garage roof. I never did it. This was a dare for the older ones and I remember one guy who jumped off, missed his footing and plunged head-long into the burn.

Whitlawburn was a good place to grow up. It did have problems, but for me it was a happy place to look back on. Nobody had much and everyone just had to get on with life. Many look at schemes and assume it's all scum who live there, but in fact it's decent folks doing their best with what's in front of them.

Today more people are financially and materially comfortable and don't rely on other's help to get by. If you're flitting you hire a van or if you need a plumber you look up Yellow Pages. Now you wouldn't think of calling a mate, but back then it was a necessity. Everyone mucked in. That's real community spirit.

A grainy newspaper image of Cathkin High which featured large in many lives.

Whitlawburn Farm, as seen from East Kilbride Road.

Newspaper photo of Whitlawburn farm and green fields.

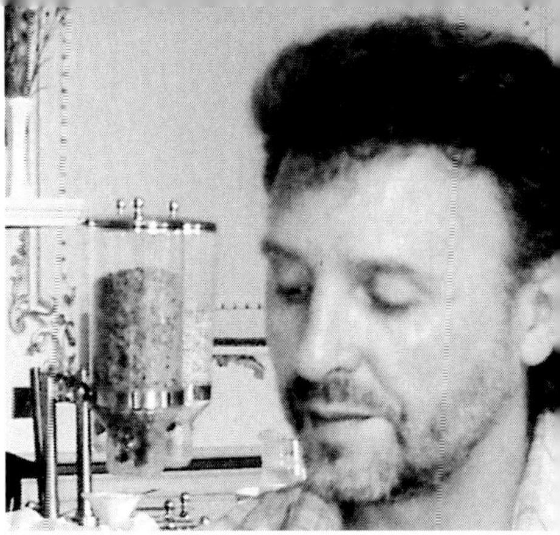

Jim Nisbet

October 1971: Rod Stewart was in the middle of a five-week run at the top of the charts with *Maggie May* and the leaves in Johnny's Woods had just turned forty shades of bronze when I first set sight on Whitlawburn.

As usual, the four o'clock bell in Westcoats Primary signalled home time. However, for the first time in my short life, I'd have to hike homewards in the drizzling rain, instead of catching the No.75 bus to Westburn.

As I trekked up the grey ribbon of a path, which back then seemed akin to an Alpine trail, the distant looming towers appeared to frown down and mock my tiring, wiry legs. Then, reaching the pinnacle of the climb, Lanarkshire Council's Promised Land abruptly burst into view on the opposite side of Western Road – a flat-roofed, prefabricated assembly of concrete and windows as far as the eye could see.

This was Whitlawburn, the focus of my world for the next seven years with Maxton Terrace at the beating heart.

Immediately, I inwardly mourned for the tidy gardens and back and front doors of Westburn Avenue, the pals I'd left behind, childhood adventures on the banks of the River Clyde, playing hide-and-seek in Redpath Brown's steelworks and make-shift football pitches chalked out on our leafy avenue. There and then, I vowed I'd be back in Westburn every weekend.

The previous night, a bulky van had delivered most of my family's belongings to Whitlawburn, and my mother, father, grandfather, and sister would finish the flitting that day, anticipating my arrival.

Surprisingly, as I entered the close the wafting scent of newness, the ambient marble effect on the walls and pristine stairs alleviated my sulk. The house was bright with a spacious kitchen, loads of cupboards and hidey-holes, a new-fangled hot-air heating system and out-sized doubled-glazed windows. Still, much effort was needed to transform this modern house into a home.

If our flat's interior was a work in progress, so too were the obvious surroundings – in essence Whitlawburn was very much a building site. From my window's panorama Lorne Terrace and Staffa Road were still under construction, the red-ash roads and pavements awaited a covering of tarmac, the barren terrain between the maisonettes longed to be landscaped and many flats were as yet unlet, casting a desolate mood over the scheme. Rumours abounded that some blocks had been built back to front, while the architect's design displayed a distinct Mediterranean influence. This probably seemed grand on the planning board, though hardly suitable for the damp, dreich Scottish climate.

But things would improve, though not overnight, and certainly not without dogged efforts from an exceptional team of local campaigners.

Friendships formed, small communities began to emerge centred round the traditional close, followed by a tenants' association, a pensioners' hut, football teams, Gala Days, and a summer Playscheme. Slowly, amenities materialised though not in order of necessity (a bookies and a pub were built before Asda appeared), lawns were laid and trees planted, play parks were put up and housing conditions improved, mainly due to years of fighting spirit and grit by Whitlawburn's tenants.

Here was leadership in action, by neighbourhood volunteers who shared a common area and mutual interest to create a colourful, thriving community amongst the planners' monotone towers and bland concrete blocks – a stark contrast to the green hills of Donegal where I now reside.

Whilst transcribing the remarkable recordings of Whitlawburn's first families, the 'ex-pats' and present residents' experiences, I wandered merrily through their memories which, in turn, awakened my senses to numerous reminiscences.

There were voices, names and faces; the echoing chimes of Pelino's and De Marco's ice-cream vans; the aroma of burning candles drifting from dens in cellars where many a ghost story was told or romance kindled; frosty November nights and icy slides down the tunnel; sounds of screams and jeers as some poor fellow fell in the burn while playing doakies; the sight of 20-a-side football matches up the Coosie; the red glow reflecting on the evening sky from the molten steel at Clydebridge beaming into your bedroom; the early morning shouts of "Sunday papers!" disturbing a hundred hangovers, compliments of a lively session in the Bel-Air, and images of the Maxton Bombers congregated at the corner of Morven Road, playing cards, jesting and nattering to all hours.

This was the stage where I acted out my youth. And such an environment can't fail to leave an indelible mark on any young mind; thus, I'll never forget the fond friends and families who made those years spent in the scheme worthy of note.

But the march of time brings change. My old house is no more; Maxton Terrace - along with Aron, Rona, Morven, Staffa, and Lorne - was demolished without ceremony in 2019, making way for a new chapter in Whitlawburn's story.

Which now begs a very important personal question – where the hell are they going to hang my plaque?!!

ICE CREAM
MADDIE

Marie Dornan and Margaret Kelly

I was about six years old when I moved to Whitlawburn in 1970.

My mother originally came from Colebrooke Street and my dad lived round the corner from her in Park Street. Many of the people who stayed in the other back streets (Mansion St, Bridge St and Church St) of Cambuslang moved to Whitlawburn. You felt safe because of that.

After marrying, my parents got a house in Somervell Street next to Hoover. My mother told me that the rent was only 37s. 6d. Following a short spell in Canada, they returned to Silverbanks, before applying to the council for a house in Whitlawburn.

No. 63 Bute Tower was a lovely house and brand new. There was a "steamie" for washing clothes down on the ground floor. My mum thought this was wonderful. Everyone took their turn at cleaning the landing and there was always a caretaker around to help out.

Neighbours were always there if you needed them - you only had to chap a door, and even though we were literally living on top of each other, it wasn't overbearing. There was a strong sense of community and I remember going to parties at Christmas and New Year in neighbours' flats.

Halloween was also great. There were millions of us kids going up and down the towers and even to the Castle on East Kilbride Road, dragging bags of goodies with us.

When Wimbledon was on we'd chalk out courts in the car park and play tennis. If it was raining, pals would play on the landings.

Sometimes we'd go round the doors asking for empty ginger bottles. If they had the lid on them you could trade the bottles for sweets to ice-cream vans such as De Marco and Pelino. My mum would frequently send me down with a soup bowl to get it filled with ice-cream, but because we lived on the 11th floor, I had to run down all the flights of stairs as I didn't have time to wait for the

Marie, her mum and dad, and sister - Margaret, Billy, Maire and Debbie.

Marie , Debbie and mum Margaret.

Margaret and Billy, Marie's mum and dad in earlier years.

Marie Kelly and Debbie.

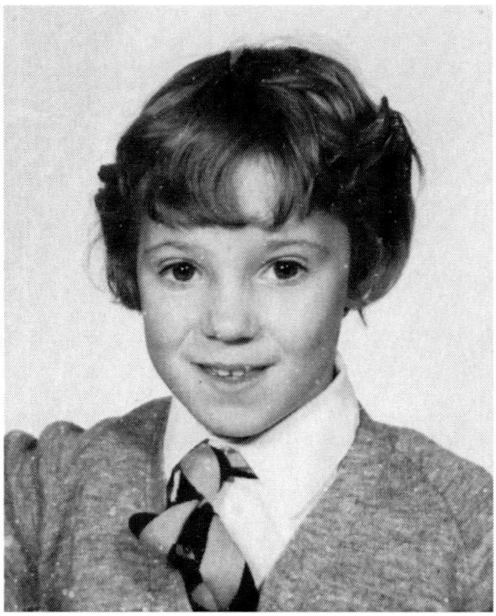

Marie – school photo.

lift. By the time I'd reached the ground floor the van would've often disappeared. It would drive me insane. It was the same when I got older. Whenever I phoned a taxi, the driver would be pulling away with me trying to run after it with my high heels on, screaming like an eejit!

Living on the 11th floor was handy on cold mornings. I'd sit at the hot air vent of the central heating system eating my corn flakes with my school uniform on, then watch from the window for the bus coming from Fernhill. It had to still pass through Cathkin and Springhall, so I knew I'd plenty of time to get down eleven floors to the bus stop outside Cathkin High School. Can you imagine any six year old going on a bus themselves nowadays?

It would have been a whole lot easier if I'd gone to St. Anthony's in Springhall - just a short trip through the underpass - but my mum and dad had gone to St. Bride's in Cambuslang so it was decided that I was going there too.

I could also have attended Cathkin High which was about ten steps from Bute Tower, but no, I had to go to Trinity High, probably because of the whole Catholic/Protestant thing, even though Cathkin High was considered non-denominational. So, instead I had a 40-minute troop home through the Public Park from Gateside everyday with my friend Janice Kielty from Aron Terrace. Sometimes on warm days we'd stop at the shops in Kirkhill and buy frozen orange jubilees.

It was worse when Trinity High moved to the new-build school in Eastfield. Then I had to walk along Langlea Road and down Hawthorn Walk in hail, rain and snow. It was freezing, and back then female pupils weren't allowed to wear trousers as a part of the uniform and our legs were always freezing.

My mum hated the lifts. She was always getting stuck much to the amusement of the neighbours who'd hear her cries for help. I think mum was glad when she moved to Kirkhill in later years to escape her fear of lifts.

All in all, I stayed in Whitlawburn for around 17 years. There were nicer places, but it wasn't the worst place to grow up. It was what it was and what I knew at that time. I was quite happy there and have good memories.

Rear of 1 Aron Terrace.

Molly Keery

Yes, I lived in Whitlawburn from 1971 for 42 years.

I originally came from Westburn Farm. I've stayed in Cambuslang all my life. Well, after I got married I was offered a house in Whitlawburn and that was it. I stayed there until I moved about 6 years ago.

I miss Whitlawburn I do, funny enough. Though I don't know if I'd like to go back now, but if we could get the original people back together again – yes, I would. When I first moved there, I thought I was in a mansion! The kitchens were big, the bathrooms were great, everything was so new and it was lovely meeting new friends.

I lived in Rona Terrace, right on Western Road at the bus stop and the tunnel. There were stunning views right over to the Campsies, until they built the houses opposite. I stayed in the end close of the first block – No. 21, underneath the McClearys.

When Asda opened it was a big fanfare for the people of Whitlawburn. The manager was standing at the door shaking hands with everyone as they entered. It was very clean and smart, but like everything else, it changed.

Prior to Asda being built the women had to go by bus to Cambuslang, or even Rutherglen and East Kilbride, and humph the messages up the road, so it was godsend having the shop, particularly for all those young families.

I had three children and they attended the local schools.

They went to Busheyhill at first, then Aitken Primary and Cathkin High School. I attended Gateside. I'm very disappointed to see that it's been demolished. It was such a lovely red sandstone building. There's now an Aldi store on the site. I remember your mum from school but we weren't in the same class.

In Whitlawburn I was involved in the Playscheme. Originally it was Lanarkshire Council that started it, then Glasgow District took it over and then it was under South Lanarkshire Council.

I became involved just through hearing others talk about it. I was asked to help out, so I said I'll give it a try and that was me enrolled – they wouldn't let me go again! There were people getting paid as well as us volunteers, but they would tell the kids what to do and a lot of the older ones would rebel against this, whereas we would talk to them and say: "Do you fancy doing this or that?" - and they'd do it quite the thing. There was a lot who came later on from Springhall and Cathkin.

When I first moved up to Whitlawburn there was a lot of fisticuffs at times between the new scheme and Cathkin and Springhall, but this encouraged the schemes to amalgamate. My son could walk into Springhall and Cathkin and he would be all right. That's one of the reasons why I started in the Playscheme – because of the fighting and if they knew me they wouldn't do anything to him. I still see some of these boys in the Main Street and they stop to speak to me and say: "Remember me? I went to Playscheme!"

My role was helping out in Arts and Crafts and things like that. We did have a few lessons in Hamilton College covering things like swimming and basketball and other activities you could entail in the community, though we didn't have the facilities initially. The Playscheme was only in Langlea Road for a few years then it moved to Cathkin High School.

There was a timetable which began in the mornings from 10 o'clock to 12.00, then in the afternoon from 1pm to 4. It didn't cost and that was why it was so popular.

When the centre was in Langlea, it was a centre for those with special needs and when the Playscheme went for day trips somewhere we travelled on the Dalton buses. Dalton was the name of a school for pupils with special needs. It was on the main Hamilton road between Halfway and Blantyre and these were the grey buses that collected these children and took them to Dalton. We were probably the first to include everyone, but that was just how people lived then.

The Playscheme was such a positive influence and it gave you an interest in the place and you kept in touch with people round about. That was the key, as it created a sort of identity.

It was Betty and her husband George Lindsay from Maxton Terrace and myself who were the backbone of it – others came and went. It just stopped – just fell away. I think it was the funding and that was that.

It definitely made a difference to the community. I mean, that's why it started in the first place because there was nothing for the kids to do except play on climbing frames and swings or go down the burn. They were frustrated and this caused fights between schemes. I think the Playscheme really helped as they were all brought together.

For a wee while I was involved in the Tenants' Association right at the start. That's when Whitlawburn was one housing estate – it wasn't the two.

When people first moved up there they were so proud of their place. They used to keep it clean and the closes were all swept and mopped. There was a rota. One neighbour did one week and vice versa. Everyone took their turn at doing the back close, the rubbish chute and the "midgie room", but when the original tenants gradually moved out and others replaced them, some of them refused to do the stairs. That's why it's in the state it is now.

I moved away because I lived on the third floor and thought I'm getting too old for these stairs. Then I was approached by people from Amenity Housing to see if I wanted a house. The council said it was adequate enough for me as I was living in a four apartment all by myself, so I moved in here and thought I was in a doll's house compared to Whitlawburn!

I enjoyed my time in Whitlawburn from the start. Once you got in and settled you met up with all sorts of people, made a lot of friends, especially in the Playscheme. In later years it deteriorated something terrible, but there were a lot of great memories.

Just built - another grainy newspaper photograph of houses in Whitlawburn, a place when engendered many happy memories of childhoods, and later lives, spent there.

Morag Donaldson

I lived at No. 11 Aron Terrace, second close, first floor up on the right. It was a four-apartment with three bedrooms. We'd came from Springhall, but it was only a two-bedroom, so we needed a bigger house.

We flitted in December 1971 when I was ten years old, my brother Adam was six and my big sister Jean was 14.

We moved in on the very same night as our neighbours below, Allister and Janette Simpson. Unfortunately, they had an identical blue van for their flitting. It was a dark night and we were constantly running in and out, getting each other's belongings mixed up. It was very confusing! We were the only neighbours in the close until after the New Year.

It was all very exciting with all these new-fangled accessories, fitted kitchen, new plug points, new floorboards. There were even windows that opened up the way, and windows that opened sideways. The closes had a marble effect on the stairs and there was a fancy rubbish chute in between each landing. My mother loved her house in Whitlawburn.

We had beautiful views from our front windows – there was nothing but green fields between us and the Cathkin Braes and the East Kilbride road. I can remember it all so vividly.

I soon got together with a new group of friends from Aron Terrace – Anne Marie McAuley (3rd close) Karen Kielty (4th close) and Charlotte Coyle (last close). There was also Janice Coyle from Gartmore Terrace and Lynn Donaldson and Grace Gunn, who were both in my class at Loch Primary over in Springhall. Janice and Anne Marie were winners of the Miss Whitlawburn contest in the early 70s!

We played various games like rounders and kick the can on the square, hide-and-seek in the fields, beds and ropes.

Beds was the English equivalent of hopscotch. There were two versions – one with nine squares in a grid, the other consisted of a line, both chalked on the pavement. You pushed an old shoe polish tin filled with stones into a square then hopped along on one leg trying not to land on a line.

Again, there were various versions of playing ropes. Elastic bands were threaded through to make a rope. Then two girls stood with legs apart holding the elastics round their ankles while the other girls would jump in and out. It was easy at first, but then the rope was raised to the knees, hips and eventually the shoulders, where you had to do handstands or cartwheels to get over. I never could do them, so I just used to hold the bands.

Another game meant borrowing someone's washing line rope. Holding a short rope two girls would turn or coil the rope while another skipped in the middle. With a longer rope, anything up to a dozen girls could jump in and out singing rhymes such as, "In and out those dusty bluebells, in and out those dusty bluebells, in and out those dusty bluebells, I am the master!"

We'd also play doakies at the burn. A doakie was a sort of dare where a route was laid out along the burn. It started with an easy jump across the burn and got harder as we snaked down the burn. If someone backed out or landed in the burn they were out of the game. Many times, I got my feet wet and can still feel the mud sticking between my toes.

The boys would sometimes build dams and we'd cool our feet in the burn on hot summer days. Our mother used to shout out the window: "Watch the rats," but I don't think anyone ever saw one.

That's how we amused ourselves. It's not like today, my mother was too busy working in the Hoover or doing her housework. We had to get out and play and not be under her feet.

When the Asda supermarket opened it was like manna from heaven. Before that different vans came around the scheme selling groceries, fish and ice-cream. My pal's mother, Mrs Kielty used to send us to Curley's in Cambuslang for her messages. She had loads of weans and I think it was cheaper to send us both rather than watch her kids, as they would've wrecked the house!

Another fond memory was the visit of the Kielty clan to our house to watch the royal wedding of Princess Anne in 1973, because we had a colour telly.

I used to babysit for half of Whitlawburn. Most of the three-apartments were occupied by young couples with kids. I loved babies and pushing prams and taking them for a hurl until they fell asleep. It was also a good way of making money when you were a teenager.

After leaving Loch Primary, I attended Cathkin High School from 1973-77.

(Cathkin High School was the result of the Munn and Dunning Report. Sir James Munn was the headmaster of the school in the 70s.)

Cathkin High was arranged into six separate houses in three blocks – Kelvin and Livingstone; Telford and Stevenson; Napier and McIntosh - each with their own community room. As well as the main Education and Administration Departments which had a library and theatre there were separate Science, Music, Technical and Art Departments. The PE block was huge with three gyms, a games hall and a swimming pool which I loved.

After leaving school I lost touch with my school friends but did widen my network. I worked as a machinist in Laird Porch in East Kilbride before training as a chef. I then worked in Clydebridge Steelworks and various hotels in places such as Arran and even had a stint in the Falklands. I now live in the Highlands with my husband Frank.

Growing up in Whitlawburn has left me with a patchwork quilt of memories: long hot summers and sitting out the front of the close; the shows coming to Whitlawburn and George McCrae singing *Rock your Baby*; the Miss Whitlawburn contest; bat the ball, rounders and all the Kieltys in our living room watching the royal wedding. Everyone was involved with everyone else. It was a happy place.

Davy Tannahill with Patsy Ross (Janice's mother-in-law.)

Nessie Tannahill and her oldest daughter, Janine.

Nessie Tannahill

My husband David and I were not long married when we moved to Whitlawburn after returning from Luton, in December 1971. We were the first tenants in Kintore Tower and lived in No. 34 where we had our first daughter, Janine.

When we first arrived in Kintore the housing conditions were atrocious – doors and windows weren't fitted correctly and the lifts frequently broke down causing much inconvenience. It was then David got the idea of forming a Tenants' Association. This brought together other enthusiastic residents such as Robert Kielty, Aron Terrace; Susan Brownlee, Morven Road; Betty Lindsay, Maxton Terrace; Molly Keery, Rona Terrace; John Edgar, Maxton Terrace and Irene Brandham, to name but a few.

David and I felt Kintore Tower wasn't a child-friendly home, so we did a mutual exchange with someone in Morven Road. Here we had a beautiful big kitchen, decent-sized bedrooms, our own cellar, a drying green and we could look out the window to keep an eye on the kids playing.

Our next-door-neighbours were an English couple, Ann Marie and Grenville, who worked for South Lanarkshire Council. They were also members of the Tenants' Association and they arranged for a lorry-load of trees to be planted around Morven Road and surrounding courts as part of the "Plant a Tree in '73" initiative of that year.

The Tenants' Association campaigned on various issues to better the scheme. Bunty Gunn, the local councillor, was involved in a lot of our concerns, though she was considered by many to be like Maggie Thatcher before Thatcher was Thatcher!

We managed to get a football pitch set up in a field at the top of Morven Road, nicknamed the Coosie and held a few galas there. There was even a Miss Whitlawburn competition with the winner selected by the *Rutherglen Reformer's* photographer. Anderson, the Coal Merchants supplied a lorry for the float.

Before Asda was built Whitlawburn's shopping needs were served by a few grocery vans. So, the Tenants' Association fought for a couple of shops as most residents had to travel to Cathkin, Cambuslang or Safeway in Burnside for their weekly messages. The local women loved Asda and it gave much needed employment at a time when jobs were hard to come by. It drew customers from all over the place - the car park was always full.

David and a few others would stand outside Asda's doors on a Saturday and sell the *Morning Star*. However, the management of Asda weren't too chuffed and called the police on several occasions when they began collecting money during the Miners' Strike of 1984-5 and calling on customers to boycott South African products in protest at the country's apartheid laws. Don't think I tasted a good orange for years!

Davy Tannahill and Robert Ross (Janice's husband) selling the Morning Star during an Anti-Apartheid Movement stall outside Asda in Whitlawburn.

The Tenants' Association hired buses to attend demonstrations and events outside the County Buildings, Hamilton. We also organised a Rent Strike in 1976, as we felt the council weren't doing necessary repairs or even cutting the grass. It lasted for about nine months and many people struggled. It landed a lot of tenants in arrears including myself as my husband David thought I was putting the money in the bank which clearly wasn't the case!

The *Whitlawburn News* was set up by the Tenants' Association. David bought a wee portable typewriter and would sit in our kitchen and lay it out. Then I would drive down to a chap in Dumbarton to print it. People would hand in snippets of news and whenever election time came around, councillors and even the local MP wanted a mention in it. Local shops would advertise in the *Whitlawburn News* and that helped cover the cost. It was free and we used to give kids a bundle of leaflets to distribute it through Whitlawburn's letterboxes. It worked out really well and ran for a long time.

Betty Lindsay with a few helpers initiated a Playscheme for Whitlawburn's youngsters in Whitlawburn Annex, though it was restricted to the use of the hall as the school had previously suffered substantial fire-damage.

Cathkin High School was a community school. Margaret Smellie was the community officer and she suggested there was a room available to start up a toddlers' group. Eventually, the Playscheme also moved to Cathkin High where we got the use of the gym halls and swimming pool. This ran for a period of six weeks during the school summer holidays from 10am-12noon and 2-4pm. The Playscheme was also extended to take in children from neighbouring schemes of Springhall and Cathkin.

The buses from the Dalton, a local specials-needs school, were put at our disposal. We were also given public transport travel passes for two adults and eight children. The Playscheme organised trips all over the place which was fantastic for those kids who hadn't even been out of the schemes.

It was mainly funded by grants from Glasgow City Council who also supplied a couple of community workers to assist local volunteers. There was a café in the school, so I used to stock it with sweets, crisps and drinks from a cash and carry. We made quite a wee profit which was ploughed back into the Playscheme. Money was also raised from jumble sales and the likes and even Asda and the Tenants' Association gave donations to help the wheels roll along.

However, as years went by volunteers became hard to get and we eventually had to pay towards the use of premises and cover the janitor's wages during the summer holidays. We just couldn't afford it and like many things it just fell away.

Our family eventually moved to Springhall in 1978, as I wanted my own back and front door. But living in Whitlawburn was a memorable time. We were all young, it was my first house, I had loads of friends and it was great community.

Betty Lindsay at Davy and Nessie's Silver Wedding anniversary.

Stewart Walker

I was born 1966 in Beckford Lodge, Hamilton. My mum, dad and elder brother had lived in Singapore but came home prior to my birth. My life's journey began in Vicar's Walk, Cambuslang where I lived with my grandparents.

My mum was from Cambuslang. My gran was one of the MacIntosh clan and the family business was MacIntosh the Bakers which some people of a certain age may still remember. My father hailed from Ardrishaig and spent many years at sea with the Royal or Merchant Navy.

The first real family home I knew was No. 61 Arran Tower, Whitlawburn. We moved there around 1970-71 and were among the first residents in the tower block. Everyone soon got to know each other and I grew up with many good friends including Jim Stevenson, Thomas Reid and David and William Torrance who lived next door.

Pals would chap the door at first light and we would be out until the street lights came on. We'd play on our bikes and skateboards, steal prams to make bogeys and foray up into the fields which is where I suffered my first-ever bout of hayfever. I also went to the Playscheme during the school holidays and went on some brilliant bus runs. There was no sitting about in the house – you were always outside making your own entertainment.

I remember watching the Asda being built which was another great playground for us young ones. Health and Safety all went out the window back then and we didn't have a care in the world.

If you wanted something to eat, you'd shout up eleven floors: "Mum, I want a piece!" So a piece was packed in a bag, thrown out the window and hit the ground like a meteor, turning to mush. But it still tasted great!

Whitlawburn.

We just loved Whitlawburn. It was a community where you could drop into parties in every house at New Year. Our neighbours, the Torrances weren't just our friends, they were like family, so much so I even called David and William's parents Aunt Lena and Uncle David. We enjoyed caravan holidays to Fife and Girvan together. Back then, there was no flying off to sunnier climes, but it was great fun and the best of times.

My mum was in the shoe trade, but also worked in the Hoover in Cambuslang for a while, as did many Whitlawburn folks. This allowed my parents to buy their first car – a 1973 Hillman Avenger, their pride and joy.

I attended Westcoats Primary School which meant a daily walk down the lane past the Bel-Air, Grenville Drive and Stewarton Drive until I reached the school. I thought when I started secondary school at Cathkin High things would be great – no long haul, just two minutes across Western Road. But it wasn't to be.

Sadly, in 1978 my gran passed away and ultimately we all moved to Croft Road to live with my grandfather and uncle. So I had to hike an even longer distance from Croft Road through the Public Park or along Brownside Road and up the brae to Cathkin High School. However, I never lost touch with my friends in Whitlawburn and at every opportunity I'd get the bike out and cycle up. These were my favourite years, but life changes and people move on.

In 1985 my parents decided to move to Burnside. By then, I'd already embarked on my working career as a television engineer, and I decided to follow in my father and brother's footsteps and join the Royal Navy. I had some superb memories and lived in Gibraltar for 18 months, but Whitlawburn was always home to me where I still had long-term family friends.

On leaving the Royal Navy in 1994 my wife and I began looking for our first home together. An interview was secured with East Whitlawburn Tenants' Association, and subsequently about an hour later an offer of a flat was made at No. 38 Rona Terrace. I was overjoyed at the thought of going back to my roots and begin my own family life in Whitlawburn just as my parents had.

We had the best of neighbours, we all looked after the close and the community spirit was fantastic. Being three floors up allowed spectacular views from our massive kitchen of the Campsie Hills and Johnny's Woods where I played as boy.

One hilarious incident I remember was getting a phone call from a double-glazing firm. I tried to explain it was a rented council flat, but they were very persistent and arranged an appointment to come and see me. So, a salesman turns up at my door and says: "I see you're interested in buying a conservatory." I burst out laughing and in a serious tone he asked why. "You've just walked up three flights of stairs in a block of flats. Where the hell am I going to put a conservatory?" I replied, to which he started screaming and shouting: "You've wasted my time! You've wasted my time!" Absolutely priceless!

Though we now live in Cairns Avenue, Cambuslang, it was still sad to see parts of East Whitlawburn being torn down. I actually had a lump in my throat when I drove by the pale blue and cream flats of Rona Terrace, as we had made so many lasting memories in that house.

But to see the place as rubble, then the Phoenix rising from the ashes gives fresh hope for the scheme. And as part of the community council, I can't wait to see the new houses completed. Whitlawburn is evolving and moving forward. There is a now a greater amount of cultural diversity with residents from countries far and wide, and Whitlawburn is returning to where it should be, the community it was in the 1970s. Young families and those starting out on married life can do what I did and go on to have amazing lives in Whitlawburn.

Darren Young

A few weeks after I was born in Rutherglen Maternity Hospital my parents moved from their home in the town's main street to Arkle Terrace, Whitlawburn. A year and a half later in May 1980, the arrival of my younger brother Derek completed our family.

As children we loved it. Growing up in Whitlawburn had everything we wanted.

One favourite game was "Wacky Races" which involved racing round the scheme on our bikes. I probably had the worst bike of all my pals, so I was usually given a 50-yard head start, but still managed to come in last. I loved my bike and its big comfy seat, but when it came to racing I hated the thing!

On summer nights mums and dads, friends and neighbours all sat outside having a wee drink while their kids ran about daft till dark. One close would play another close at rounders with everyone mucking in. Nowadays, it would be hard to replicate these memories.

Then there was the Wimbledon season at the garages. I remember some girl had actually managed to paint half a tennis court before the police arrived. It's still there as far as I'm aware. Whenever we wanted to play tennis we would just scrape the outline of the other half of the court with a brick. Then we'd borrow a couple of shopping trolleys from Asda, turn them upside down, string a washing rope across as a net cadged from a pal's mum or granny, two line judges would sit on the trolleys and the game would commence.

Another summer pastime involved filling up balloons or even an old Asda carrier bag with water from a tap at the bins, then attack and splash each other. It was all good-natured fun with no fear of getting hurt or any serious retribution that you might encounter today. There was always a real safety in the scheme, even at night, as everyone knew each other or their families.

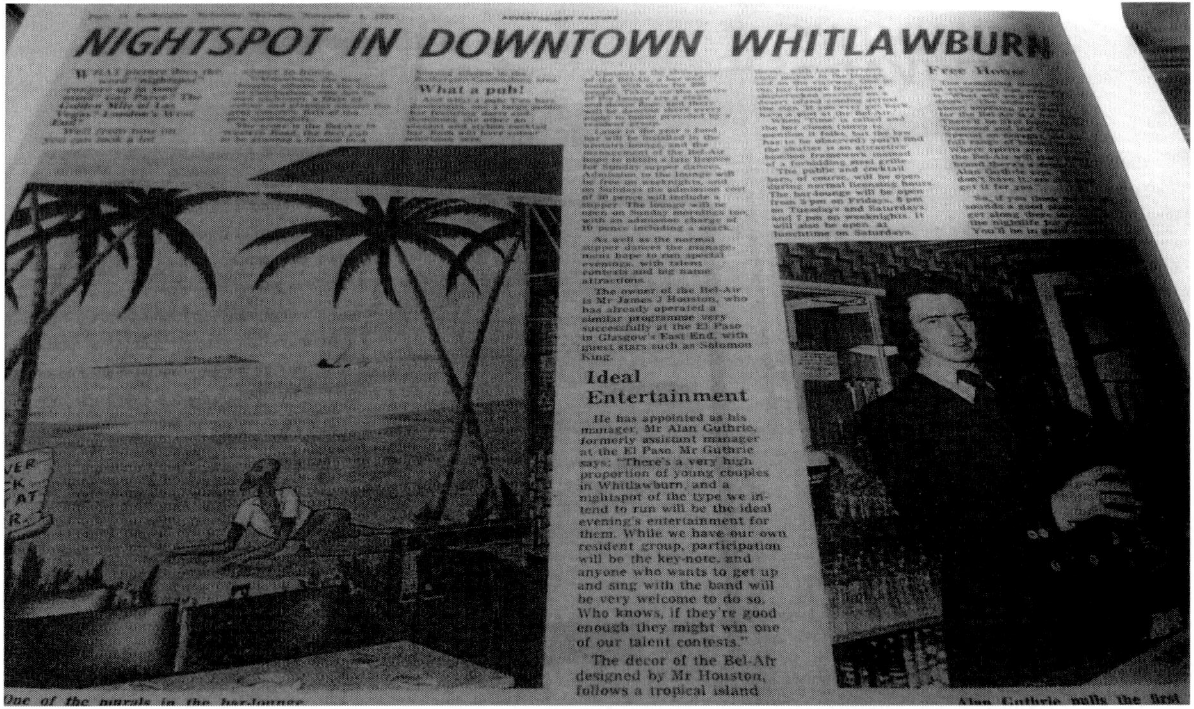

NIGHTSPOT IN DOWNTOWN WHITLAWBURN

What a pub!

As well as the normal supper dances the management hope to run special evenings, with talent contests and big name attractions.

The owner of the Bel-Air is Mr James J Houston, who has already operated a similar programme very successfully at the El Paso in Glasgow's East End, with guest stars such as Solomon King.

Ideal Entertainment

He has appointed as his manager, Mr Alan Guthrie, formerly assistant manager at the El Paso. Mr Guthrie says: "There's a very high proportion of young couples in Whitlawburn, and a nightspot of the type we intend to run will be the ideal evening's entertainment for them. While we have our own resident group, participation will be the key-note, and anyone who wants to get up and sing with the band will be very welcome to do so. Who knows, if they're good enough they might win one of our talent contests."

The decor of the Bel-Air designed by Mr Houston, follows a tropical island

Free House

Rutherglen Reformer carries article on opening of the Bel-Air in 1973.

The ice-cream vans used to halt at every road into the towers, so if you didn't catch the van at the front at Kintore Tower, five minutes later the van would be chiming round the back at Benmore.

My mum would give me 20p or 30p, but if I asked my dad for money for the van he'd give me some empty Irn Bru bottles or "glass cheques" as they were called then. Then I'd stand at the back close, ensure there were no friends about to avoid any potential embarrassment, run to the van and swap the "empties" for sweets.

I can recount so many great times in the scheme. Even now when I see *The Never Ending Story* on TV, it rekindles images of a Sunday morning in the Pensioners' hut in Morven Road with all the kids watching the latest videos. Then at the interval we'd buy juice and a pick-n-mix from the tuck shop – that's back in the day when you actually got 10 sweets for your 10p!

When we were a little bit older, the same hall played host to a disco or the "Whitlawburn Rave" as we called it. Both events were run by volunteers – people doing it not to get paid but because their children were involved.

During the school holidays the Playscheme in Cathkin High provided amusement with arts and crafts, badminton, table tennis and trampolines. I remember taking part in a massive football tournament in Helenvale Park, Parkhead. This was between other Playschemes in Glasgow and our team finished commendable runner-up against much bigger guys.

Football was always my big thing and has basically shaped my whole life. I was always walking about with a ball under my arm as a child. We were forever playing football out the front, in the drying greens, round the back at the garages and up the famous Coosie.

When I started school at Whitlawburn Annex, I'd come home at lunchtime and wolf the soup or sandwich my mum had made, straight out the front to play football until it was nearly one o'clock, then I would pick up my bag and head back to school before the bell rang, soaking with sweat. Same routine at 4pm unless mum had the tea ready, otherwise my bag was flung down, and I started kicking a ball around with everyone and anyone.

The older ones used to chap our door and ask if Derek and I would play with them. They obviously thought we were good enough. The competition was friendly, and it certainly toughened me up, and probably instilled in me a will to win, to prove myself against these bigger boys. Even today, I always do my best whatever the challenge, whether on the pitch or in football management.

When I was about seven or eight I left Whitlawburn Annex to attend Loch Primary. The walk to Springhall was quite a distance, but I was always first at school each morning as my mum started work early doors in Asda. This meant an extra 20 minutes football practice in the playground before lessons began. My dad worked offshore at the time, so I had the added responsibility of looking after Derek and locking up the house.

Returning home it was question of either taking the bus or putting the fare towards sweets. By the time 30 or 40 pupils boarded the bus at Springhall Library, we worked that by running ahead, Derek and I could beat the bus to the drop off stops outside Cathkin High School then further on at the Bel-Air pub. Again, that competitive edge was to the fore even against the school bus!

Derek and I also had a paper run when we were about 13 or 14, first distributing the *Rutherglen Reformer* and later on, an early Sunday morning rise to deliver the *Mail, People, News of the World* and the *Sunday Post*. Both jobs were good earners for youngsters at that time.

Looking back it was non-stop and my learning experiences were full of life. and I was always very fit because of all the running around.

Cathkin United was the first team I played for, I still remember the day of the trial and the legend that was Jock Barkey - he was “Mr Cathkin United” and the rock the club was built upon. Derek was also there along with every boy in the district it seemed. He was five and I was six, but there was none of this 5 or 7-a-side youngsters indulge in nowadays. We had black shorts and green and black shirts on and looked like a swarm of bees playing on a full-size pitch. I remember scoring and thinking: “Kick it high! Kick it high!” at this tiny goalkeeper whose outstretched hands could only reach halfway up towards the crossbar.

When I was ten, Aberdeen and Rangers began to show an interest in my footballing skills. This meant a trip on Mondays to train with the Dons at Strathclyde Park, Tuesday I travelled to the Astroturf pitch at Ibrox Stadium, Wednesday I’d sometimes train with Hearts and Thursday saw me at St. Anthony’s, Springhall, where it was back to jumpers for goalposts with my own team. Saturday morning was school football day with Cathkin High, hurrying home for mum’s special fry-up, then turning out for Cathkin United in the afternoon. To cap the week off, on Sunday I’d join up with the local lads playing for some Whitlawburn outfit.

Willie White was in charge of the school team at Cathkin High. A Saturday morning for Willie often meant flying around Whitlawburn and Halfway in the minibus, chapping on the door of any player who'd slept in, then rushing to get to the ground in time for kick-off. There was no such thing as mobile phones in those days!

In all those years I never missed a game, mainly thanks to my mum who was constantly picking us up and dropping us off at training and matches. She spent numerous hours sitting in car parks, drinking countless cups of tea and reading magazines while Derek and I ran about football parks. We never really appreciated the time and effort my mum put in to help Derek and I in our football careers, and it's only now, in hindsight, I realise the sacrifice she made for us both.

The very last game I played as a youngster was the final of Scottish Schools Championship which we won 1-0.

It was very sad to be leaving school and Whitlawburn, to join Aberdeen on a two-year contract. It was crazy, as within a year I had gone from playing schoolboy football and kick-a-bouts up the Coosie as a sixteen year old, to performing as "a grown up" in the Premier League and with the Scotland under-21s.

However, looking back, Whitlawburn holds so many fond memories. There was a great spirit of togetherness that you don't see today and I loved the whole community thing. All in all, those were magical times.

Darren Young has been capped for Scotland (Under 21s) and is a Scottish football coach who is manager of Scottish League One club East Fife. During his career he has played for Aberdeen, Dundee, Dunfermline Athletic and Greenock Morton. In June 2014, Darren was appointed player/manager of Scottish League Two club Albion Rovers.

The demolition of some of the flats.

Rona Terrace coming down.

WRITING WORDS LISTENING VOICES REMINISCENCES

Information

NAME	INTERVIEWED	TRANSCRIBED
Adam Donaldson	11th July 2017	29th April 2020
Alex McLaren	November 2019	4th December 2019
Alison Gilmour	8th June 2018	8th January 2020
Esther and Barbara Stewart	20th July 2018	20th February 2020
Betty Baker	Emailed 10th June 2020	–
Derek Watt	14th March 2020	30th March 2020
Eric Kielty	9th September 2020	20th October 2020
George Lindsay	22nd September 2020	30th October 2020
Geraldine McGaulley	30th July 2017	5th June 2020
Janice Ross	April 2021	–
Jessie Kielty	30th May 2018	16th May 2020
Jim Hannaway	10th November 2020	–
Jim Moore	11th June 2020	21st September 2020
Jim Nisbet	October 2020	5th November 2020
Marie Dornan and Margaret Kelly	28th July 2017	17th June 2020
Molly Keery	27th February 2018	26th November 2019
Morag Donaldson	20th July 2017	20th April 2020
Nessie Tannahill	18th June 2020	10th September 2020
Stewart Walker	26th February 2020	8th December 2020
Darren Young	27th November 2020	5th February 2021

Pale Ale sixpence. Guinness eightpence - both old money. Margaret Kelly and Anne Kielty having a whale of a time in Blackpool.

Who can you spot in this primary school photo taken around 1976.

COMMUNITY
DOAKIES
WHITLAWBURN
COOSIE
CAMBUSLANG
HOOVER

Acknowledgements

I would like to thank the following people for their support, encouragement and contribution: Jim Nisbet, Maddie Ross, James Kelly, Zen Boyd (librarian for *Reformer* article research from Rutherglen Heritage Centre at Rutherglen Library), Paul Farrell (West Whitlawburn Housing Cooperative) Graham Miller (editor of the *Rutherglen Reformer*), Cambuslang Housing Department of South Lanarkshire Council. Special thanks to Karen Ross, Dorothy and Russell Bruce and Dr. Sabine Dedenbach Salazar-Saenz. To everyone who shared their life story: Betty Baker, Adam and Morag Donaldson, Marie Dornan, Alison Gilmour, Molly Keery, Margaret Kelly, Eric Kielty, Jessie Kielty, Geordie Lindsay, Jim Moore, Geraldine McGaulley, Alex Mc Laren, Barbara and Esther Stewart, Nessie Tannahill, Stewart Walker, Derek Watt and Darren Young.

Not Miss Whitlawburn